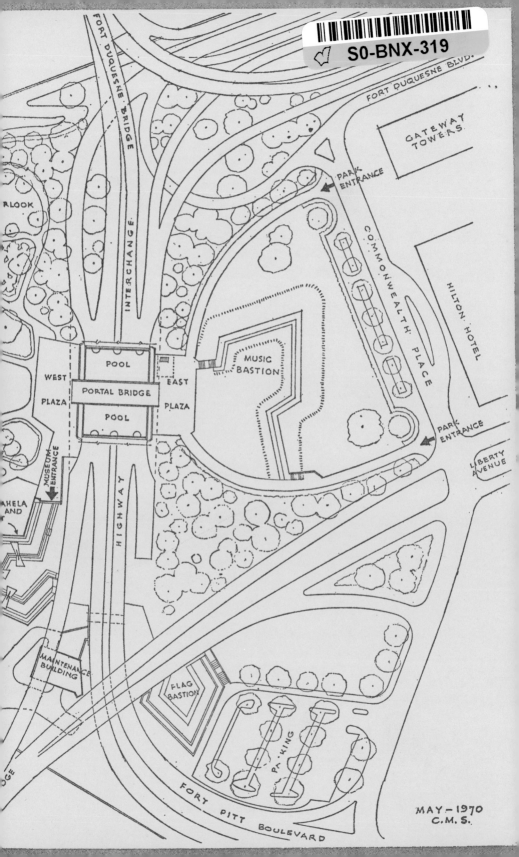

FORT DUQUESNE BRIDGE

FORT DUQUESNE BLVD.

GATEWAY TOWERS

PARK ENTRANCE

COMMONWEALTH PLACE

HILTON HOTEL

RLOOK

INTERCHANGE

MUSIC BASTION

WEST PLAZA

POOL

PORTAL BRIDGE

EAST PLAZA

POOL

MUSEUM ENTRANCE

PARK ENTRANCE

LIBERTY AVENUE

AHELA AND

HIGHWAY

MAINTENANCE BUILDING

FLAG BASTION

PARKING

GE

FORT PITT BOULEVARD

MAY—1970
C. M. S.

POINT OF EMPIRE

POINT OF EMPIRE

From their seats of power in Paris and London two foreign nations contested for the land beyond the mountains in the New World.

The native owner of this land, the Indian, was now an ally, now an enemy, but always the tragic figure in the unequal struggle.

All three were victors in their time, all losers in the end.

POINT OF EMPIRE

Conflict at the Forks of the Ohio

BY

CHARLES MORSE STOTZ

THE HISTORICAL SOCIETY OF WESTERN PENNSYLVANIA

4338 Bigelow Boulevard, Pittsburgh, Pennsylvania 15213

TABLE OF CONTENTS

LIST OF ILLUSTRATIONS

Illustrations on pages 32, 46 and 79 are reproduced from *Drums in the Forest,* by James and Stotz

Illustrations on the cover, frontispiece, pages 42 and 65 are from water-color paintings by Nat Youngblood

Illustrations on pages 90, 93, 95 and 97 are renderings by Julian E. Michele, made from the original drawings of Point State Park

All photographs are the work of Marc Neuhof of New York City, except those on pages 15, 28, 83 and 88-89 which are by Alan Perkins of Titusville, Pennsylvania, and the photograph on page 35 by Photo Associates of Pittsburgh.

FOREWORD

A FOREWORD IS defined as a "prefatory statement" and precedes a book or booklet. It always appeared to me to be an utterly useless idea. If the book is not worth its salt, no foreword can save it; and if it is really good, the foreword becomes merely frosting on the cake. It is for this latter reason I found it very difficult in all honesty to write a foreword for this account of the Fort Pitt Museum and its exhibits. It is all here, and it is magnificent.

The Fort Pitt Museum is unique as far as I know among all museums, large or small. It rests in a setting, the Commonwealth's Point Park, designed and largely developed by architect Charles M. Stotz and associates who include the distinguished landscape architect, Ralph E. Griswold. The building itself was designed by Stotz, as were the exhibits, with some help from the Pennsylvania Historical and Museum Commission staff and such expert consultants as Fred Kinsey, who was formerly with the Commission and is now with the North Museum of Franklin and Marshall College in Lancaster. Pittsburgh's Holiday Displays, headed by Harold and Raymond Yoest, constructed the cases, dioramas, and exhibits, under the direction of the architect. The Yoests contributed much by their expert craftsmanship and their extensive knowledge of period character. The decorative and informative backgrounds were painted by Joseph Hajnas.

The museum is based upon Stotz's research and writings about Fort Pitt and the forts of the French and Indian War era. In truth, it is very much his museum, and that is why this booklet is indispensable. It is an incomparably brief and graphic history of the French and Indian War in western Pennsylvania.

Much has been written by expert historians about that era in Pennsylvania and American history, but this author has added something extra. He is in his own way as much a historian as an architect and has done original research no one else has undertaken. His unique contribution, I think, is that he has made himself an authority on such things as how forts were really built and how the officers and soldiers actually lived in them. The conventional historian develops in great depth the background history of the events and the political personalities of the French and Indian War era, such as

Braddock, Forbes, and Bouquet, but it has taken Stotz to bring to life the marches, the life in the forts, and the life around the forts.

The Fort Pitt Museum is without doubt the most complete presentation of this vital era in American history ever put on display. It tells also how Pittsburgh began, for it is more than a military museum. Such a museum is needed to give Pittsburghers, adults and children alike, a greater sense of the city's roots in its past. This message is equally important for the many visitors from distant places in this country and abroad.

Because it would take far more time than the average visitor has at his or her disposal on one visit to the Fort Pitt Museum to get the full story told in the exhibits, this booklet will be of help. You will want to come back again after reading it. If you are unable to visit the Fort Pitt Museum, this booklet will provide a capsule history of the period, which is beyond compare in any other single piece of writing I know about.

S. K. Stevens, *Executive Director*
Pennsylvania Historical and Museum Commission

Harrisburg, Pennsylvania
April 15, 1970

AUTHOR'S PREFACE

THE WORLD'S first historian, Herodotus, wrote nearly 2500 years ago that he was publishing his researches ". . . , in the hope of thereby preserving from decay the remembrance of what men have done . . ." His fascinating account of the ancient world of Greece, Egypt and Persia belies the all-too-common notion that history is dry. The unquenchable curiosity and enthusiasm of these early Greeks has served as a tonic for those who would savor life to its full. As in great poetry, history mirrors the reality of life in all its ugliness and its beauty, its tragedy and its comedy.

Since the time of Herodotus man has continued unceasingly to attempt to record the story of his own region, the origin, growth and peculiar significance of his civilization. But whereas the European historian has been concerned with the layer upon layer of civilization that preceded his own, we in western Pennsylvania must begin with a relatively unoccupied wilderness of little more than 200 years ago. Except for the prehistoric Indian, of whom we have scanty knowledge, our story, when placed on the time-table of human history, began only yesterday, or rather a few moments ago.

Over such a relatively brief span one might think it would be a simple matter, in current lingo, "to tell it like it is," or was. However, a reasonably faithful portrayal of our past involves hours of patient research, known to the worker as labor on the rockpile. To achieve a definitive statement is reserved for few. Except for the fragmentary records of early missionaries and traders, we must depend almost entirely upon the military correspondence, maps and plans in the French and English archives. Few travelers went west of the mountains before 1765 and settlers were prohibited by royal edict. Like the archaeologist, who has revealed much by recovery of artifacts from the ground, the historian must delve through mountains of words to learn what truly happened and what the people and their environment were really like — and even then he can never be absolutely certain!

This museum was planned to provide a reliable synopsis of the events and personages of our region before 1800, together with an understanding of the effects of geography and environment on our place in history. From its beginning Pittsburgh has been a funnel through which currents of humanity surged westward, a fact symbolized literally and figuratively by our three great rivers that bear such beautiful Indian names: the Monongahela, the Allegheny and the Ohio. The styles of our early buildings bear evidence of this diversity of origins among our people. Pittsburgh today is enriched by a polyglot population, almost unique in our country.

Now that Pittsburgh, at long last, has a museum devoted to its early days let us hope that its citizens of so many origins will achieve a common pride in its past. The interested visitor has available to him an excellent library of our regional history. A selection of these books is listed on page 99. Here he will find a story packed with excitement, rich in anecdote and laid against a background of conflict and struggle for survival. The story is climaxed by one of the greatest migrations of history, as the people of the eastern seaboard poured across the mountains into the inland basin of America.

After more than two hundred years we can see the story in somewhat better perspective, with less tendency to gild the past or to indulge in equally perverse muckraking. However, our historical sources show that all was not good or honorable. The provincial soldier of 1758 welcomed his perilous duty in the forests of western Pennsylvania no more eagerly than does the G.I. of 1970 in the jungles of Vietnam. Military records are tarnished by accounts of mutiny and desertion. The society of Fort Pitt was crude. British military action was dilatory and inefficient. The mid-18th century government of New France was notoriously corrupt. Outrages committed on the frontier by the Indians were matched by those of the white man who double-talked as he confiscated.

On the other side of the coin are records of self-sacrifice and valor among the men and women of the frontier. There were also many persons of noble character among the Indians. Few passages in literature can match the dignity, colorful imagery, and just reasoning of the Indian orators, yet the Indian is all too often characterized as a diabolical fiend.

It is ironical that we today should possess this country, so aptly named "delectable," for which two European powers struggled long ago. Their conflict was a bitter one. In retrospect it seems picturesque to us. Their arms, their dress, their customs, their frontier forts and buildings, their grand plans for conquest as well as their informal moments of relaxation, all these things form the subject matter of the exhibits in this museum. This is the story of the French and Indian

War in what is now western Pennsylvania and the development of civilization about the frontier village of Pittsburgh before 1800.

As the medium for interpreting our historical heritage the Fort Pitt Museum is the heart of Point State Park. Although it is, in a sense, a "package" museum, employing sixty exhibits to tell a story limited in geographical area as well as in historical span, the intent of the designers was to avoid a static character. The Museum was conceived as a flexible space with a minimum of fixed partitions, readily adjustable to accommodate future accessions and concepts, and with generous space for special shows to bring freshness and renewed public appeal. The Information Center affords facilities for endless varieties of audio-visual presentations while the sales area is a center for the dissemination of educational literature and historical mementos.

As an added source of vitality the Historical and Museum Commission has established a non-profit corporation of local citizens known as the Fort Pitt Museum Associates. Working in collaboration with the curator, Rex T. Lohmann, this group will provide volunteers for many services, including the operation of the sales area, and the general promotion of Museum activities.

CHARLES MORSE STOTZ
Fellow of the American Institute of Architects

Pittsburgh, Pennsylvania
June 1, 1970

I. THE GREAT HALF-CENTURY 1750-1800

Somewhat before 1750 the headwaters of the Ohio emerged from obscurity to become, within a few years, the stage for events that made news across the ocean. This little triangle of land, formed by the Allegheny and Monongahela Rivers, was brought into sharp international focus when it became a prize of critical importance in the worldwide contest for empire between the French and the English through four years of bitter conflict.

To protect their possessions, extending inland from Quebec to New Orleans, the French here made their decisive move to intercept English westward expansion. By seizing the Virginians' little Fort Prince George in 1754 and by building Fort Duquesne on its site, the French established control of the Ohio Valley until 1758. For these four years, this little settlement was a French town that Louis XV hoped to make the permanent capital of his lands beyond the Allegheny Mountains.

The English now recognized, belatedly, that the Ohio River, born at the tip of this triangle, was the open road to the vast interior of the continent and that the nation controlling this natural highway controlled the future of the land.

After two major military expeditions, the Braddock and Forbes Campaigns, the English forced the French to destroy and abandon Fort Duquesne and proceeded to build their most substantial and costly stronghold in America. This fort was named Fort Pitt and the place "Pittsbourgh," in honor of the prime minister in London who had finally brought success to British arms.

The native Indian, whose natural rights of ownership were largely ignored, looked on with growing resentment. He chose the side which at the time appeared to serve his interests best. But when the French had been defeated and the settlers rushed in to occupy the land, the Indian unleashed the full fury of his frustration, bringing terror to the frontier until his utter defeat in 1794.

The settlement about Fort Pitt grew slowly because of the restrictions of continual conflict and unrest. The very geographical circumstances that made the Forks of the Ohio a coveted military prize likewise destined the little village of Pittsburgh soon to assert its importance as the head of river travel to the inland basin of America.

1

By 1800 the seeds of a great city had taken root. The hills with their rich coal seams, readily accessible from the broad rivers that formed the head of navigation to the interior of the land, were the source of Pittsburgh's ever-increasing eminence in transportation, commerce and industry.

The young city is portrayed at various stages in its development in Exhibit 25. Exhibit 27 carries the story up to the period of industrial strife in the late 1800's. Various aspects of commerce and industry at the turn of the century appear in Exhibits 28A through 28E. Except for the above variations the Museum Story terminates at 1800.

II. A MUSEUM WITHIN THE RAMPARTS

It was inevitable that the people of Pittsburgh would eventually accomplish that which they had long sought — a suitable memorial at the Point. After 150 years of frustration this desire has been consummated in the creation of Point State Park, as described in Part V of this book. A major and most perplexing problem faced the designers of the park, in finding how to build an inconspicuous building in which to receive the public, provide offices and related facilities, an information center, storage areas and, most important, museum exhibits to portray the highlights of the momentous first fifty years.

The original park plans, made in 1945, included a modern structure to house the museum exhibits. The architect, who was also serving as historian, was among the first to agree that the broad sweep of the park should not be interrupted by buildings, even though interior museum space was required. Both purposes were accomplished by creating a large space within the Monongahela Bastion which was to be restored on its original site. There remained two problems to solve. This Bastion was originally a solid mound of earth, without the masonry facing of the eastern fort front. Since it would obviously be impossible to maintain an earth front on a permanent building, it was decided to reconstruct the Monongahela Bastion with the same masonry ramparts used on the eastern side of the fort. There was ample space within the Bastion for museum purposes. The construction is of heavy concrete supporting four feet of earth above.

The completely irregular shape of the Monongahela Bastion, dictated by the plan of Fort Pitt made by Lieutenant Elias Meyer in 1761, was faithfully followed by the architect. The odd shape of the interior led to much study to provide a practical plan, without sacrificing aesthetic considerations. The involved arrangement of the sixty exhibits may be seen in the cut-away view, illustration p. 5. To further complicate matters it was mandatory that the cases be designed and put under contract before the exhibits they were to contain had been determined.

Description of the Interior

The visitor enters through a vestibule that is served by a gift shop and the office of the caretaker of the Blockhouse, and thence into

3

the William Pitt Memorial Hall. This hall is designed with a widening effect to create a climax at the curving wall at the end, upon which will be placed a mural painting, 55 feet wide and 12 feet high. The brilliant glass mosaic floor panels depicting the soldier, settler, trader, missionary, Indian and riverman were designed by Harry Jackson, muralist and sculptor. The 15-foot-wide circular enclosure in the center of the hall contains a model of Fort Pitt and its immediate environs. A spoken description may be heard by lifting the earphones that hang on the enclosing rail.

The arms of William Pitt are executed in glass mosaic on the floor at the entrance to the Memorial Hall. Because of the difficulty in obtaining a correct version of Pitt's arms, the College of Arms in London was commissioned to prepare a colored drawing of authentic character. (See reproduction on the back of the book cover.) The frieze of the eastern wall of the Memorial Hall contains the famous statement made by George Washington when he visited the Point on November 22, 1753. ". . , I spent some Time in viewing the Rivers, and the Land in the Fork; which I think extremely well situated for a Fort, . ." And on the western wall an extract from a letter written by General John Forbes to Prime Minister William Pitt. "Pittsburgh, 27th November 1758. . . I have used the freedom of giving your name to Fort Du Quesne, . ."

From the Memorial Hall one gains access to the administrative offices and the board room. Upon entering the museum area one finds on his left the entrance to an Information Center or meeting room with seats for eighty-four persons. This will be used as an information center for lectures, film presentations and demonstrations. Regular visitation will be arranged for school groups. The Bastion contains a delivery room, work and storage area, heating and air conditioning facilities, a work-in-progress space and a small gallery for traveling shows and special exhibitions. (See the museum layout inside the back cover.)

How the Project Was Accomplished

It may be of interest here to explain the working arrangements for the accomplishment of this project. The General State Authority, acting for the Pennsylvania Historical and Museum Commission, executed a professional agreement in 1966 with Stotz, Hess and Mac-Lachlan, architects, to design, place under contract, and supervise the construction of the exhibits for the Fort Pitt Museum. The immediate

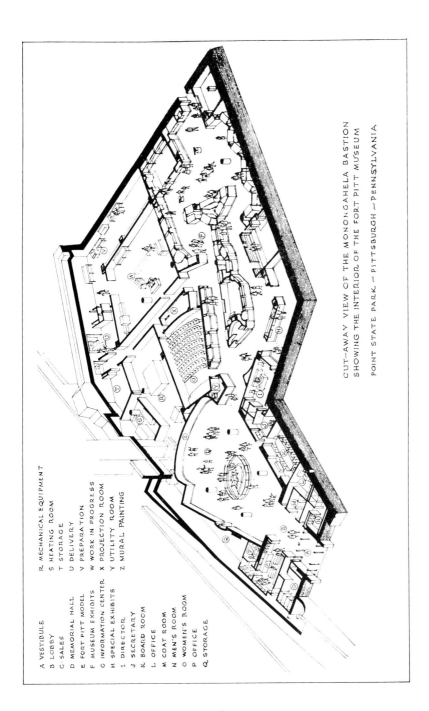

A VESTIBULE
B LOBBY
C SALES
D MEMORIAL HALL
E FORT PITT MODEL
F MUSEUM EXHIBITS
G INFORMATION CENTER
H SPECIAL EXHIBITS
I DIRECTOR
J SECRETARY
K BOARD ROOM
L OFFICE
M COAT ROOM
N MEN'S ROOM
O WOMEN'S ROOM
P OFFICE
Q STORAGE

R MECHANICAL EQUIPMENT
S HEATING ROOM
T STORAGE
U DELIVERY
V PREPARATION
W WORK IN PROGRESS
X PROJECTION ROOM
Y UTILITY ROOM
Z MURAL PAINTING

CUT-AWAY VIEW OF THE MONONGAHELA BASTION
SHOWING THE INTERIOR OF THE FORT PITT MUSEUM

POINT STATE PARK ~ PITTSBURGH ~ PENNSYLVANIA

5

direction of the work was assigned to Charles M. Stotz, who recommended that a negotiated contract be made with Holiday Displays. This was done by The General State Authority. Harold and Raymond Yoest, who had immediate direction of the work for Holiday Displays, and Stotz had worked together some years before on the exhibits for the Fort Ligonier Museum which have attracted favorable nationwide attention.

The successful prosecution of this type of work requires close and continuous collaboration between architect and contractor. In this project the architect has been required to go beyond the design of the building and the cases and rooms that contain the exhibits; he has acted in the capacity of curator in developing the historical story line to suit the sequence of cases, rooms and dioramas, write captions and narrate scripts for mechanical recording, do historical research and prepare scale drawings of the full-size rooms, fort models and general design of the exhibits themselves. The Yoest brothers have contributed much from their long experience in museum preparation, craftsmanship, model and diorama construction and study of historical costume, arms, implements and the like.

The architect organized an historical advisory committee chosen from the staff of the Historical and Museum Commission and the Point Park Steering Committee of the Allegheny Conference on Community Development, consisting of the following persons: The late Stanton Belfour, Point Park Steering Committee; J. Duncan Campbell, Pennsylvania Historical and Museum Commission; John W. Harpster, Director, Historical Society of Western Pennsylvania, W. Fred Kinsey, Consultant, Curator North Museum, Franklin and Marshall College; William N. Richards, Director of the Bureau of Museum of the Pennsylvania Historical and Museum Commission.

Contributions for purchases of materials, including artifacts and models, have been made by the Buhl Foundation, The Richard King Mellon Foundation and the Pittsburgh Foundation.

The author gratefully acknowledges permission to quote some passages from his article "Point State Park" that appeared in *The Carnegie Magazine* for January 1964.

Pittsburgh has always lacked a historical museum. It is to be hoped that these exhibits will stimulate an interest in the fascinating early aspects of the founding of our civilization and that the visitor will be induced to seek more for himself. As an aid in this effort, a short bibliography has been supplied on page 99. The basic source material upon which any dependable historical writing must be based is contained in the archives to be found in America and Europe. These authorities have been consulted in the design and preparation of the some sixty exhibits contained in the museum.

Of first importance are the *Bouquet Papers,* a mine of information comprised of British military correspondence which reveals the true nature of wilderness warfare and the colorful personalities involved. The *Contrecoeur Papers* deal with the invasion of the Ohio country by the French and the building of their forts from Lake Erie to the Point. Research also involved study of the Indian and his relations with the European invaders as well as archaeological studies of the Indians who lived near the Point 3,000 years ago. To portray the arms and armament, uniforms and everyday articles of the soldiers of the armies involved extensive research. The acquisition of artifacts was made possible through a grant by the Richard King Mellon Foundation and the model of Fort Pitt by a grant from the Buhl Foundation. The costs of designing and building the exhibits were covered by appropriations of the General State Authority.

From these materials the panorama of our place in history is presented in as definitive a manner as could be managed, utilizing modern museum techniques rather than methods more suitable to books. Exhibits include a mixture of full-scale rooms with mannequins, interpretive displays of artifacts, small-scale lifelike dioramas, models and drawings of the forts, film presentations and spoken narratives.

The exhibits are arranged in chronological sequence with variety of character to maintain freshness and interest. The cases are set to accommodate the very irregular floor plan of the bastion and provide ever-changing vistas, yet maintain comfortable clearance for visitor circulation. At the halfway point a generous open space contains a bench for relaxation. (See the plan inside the back cover.) The captions provide a consecutive historical narrative intended for the adolescent or adult who comes with an awareness of the general historical background and who, it is hoped, will be stimulated to learn for himself more about the local history.

The building, cases and exhibits were conceived, designed and built in Pittsburgh by Pittsburghers devoted to the task of providing our city with a kind of museum it has so long lacked. The Fort Pitt Museum may be regarded as a supplement and conclusion to the story told in the Fort Ligonier Museum with its unrivaled collection of French and Indian War artifacts taken from the ground there.

III. THE STORY TOLD BY THE EXHIBITS

This booklet and its illustrations form a condensed summary of the story told in the Fort Pitt Museum. A plan showing the arrangement and titles of the exhibits is reproduced on the end paper inside the back cover. This plan, together with the list of illustrations, will enable the museum visitor to place himself in the museum. All cases and exhibits are identified by numbers which agree with those given in the following pages.

1. Contest for Empire — The French and British at the Forks

The first exhibit seen on leaving the William Pitt Memorial Hall is the theme of the museum. Flag bearers of the British and French armies are ranged on each side of a center panel within which is seen the prize they sought, the Forks of the Ohio. In contrast with their colorful uniforms and flags and the symbols of their old cultures, St. Paul's in London and Notre Dame in Paris, the half-naked Indian stands within his native forest, musket menacingly raised. The panel in the foreground of the case contains a caption which sums up the fortunes of these three figures in the drama that was enacted in mid-18th century (see frontispiece). This caption reads:

> From their seats of power in Paris and London two foreign nations contested for the land beyond the mountains in the New World. The native owner of this land, the Indian, was now an ally, now an enemy, but always the tragic figure in the unequal struggle. All three were victors in their time, all three losers in the end.

2. The View West—The Mysterious Country Beyond the Mountains

A relief map extending westward to the Forks of the Ohio shows how the country seemed to the English and French colonists in mid-18th century from the eastern seaboard. A narration is heard through earphones. The possessions of the two countries are illuminated in separate colors by "black light" while the army routes light up as the narration proceeds.

The Ohio River and the country about it are quite familiar to us today but this river was practically unknown in the early 1700's. It was almost mid-century before the Ohio River was located and recognized

8

as the natural highway to the inland basin of America. When at last the French and British grasped the strategic importance of this key to the ownership of the continent, both nations claimed the Ohio Valley and sought to establish possession of its headwaters at the junction of the Allegheny and Monongahela Rivers.

Maps are almost always shown with the north at the top. But this map is turned toward the west, on its side so to speak, to show better the approach from the English and French settlements east of the Appalachian ranges. The frontiersmen called these "the endless mountains." To help you orient yourself, modern Pennsylvania is shown in outline.

The English colonies, shown in red, stretched in a thin line along the Atlantic Coast; the French possessions, shown in blue, extended from the Gulf of St. Lawrence, through the lakes and the Illinois country to the Gulf of Mexico. The land of the dominant Indians, the Iroquois, shown in green, formed a barrier as formidable as the mountains. Remaining in shadow is the no-man's-land at the Forks of the Ohio, the prize in this contest for empire.

The French reached the Ohio by a natural water route which extended from Montreal, through the St. Lawrence River, Lake Ontario, Lake Erie, French Creek and the Allegheny River. While the French had a great advantage in this water route, it was over 700 miles long and was often closed by ice in the winter. There were also difficult portages around Niagara Falls and from Lake Erie to French Creek. However, the French successfully occupied the Forks of the Ohio in 1754.

The English routes were shorter but required slow, arduous travel by land over rough military paths cut through dense forests and obstructed by many mountains. The first route extended from Williamsburg, Virginia, to the Potomac River. From here the path had led over the mountains for 125 miles and then paralleled the Youghiogheny and Monongahela Rivers to the Point. This route was followed by Braddock in 1755. His defeat left the Forks in French hands for another three years.

The second English route extended from Philadelphia to the Susquehanna River and from there about 200 miles over the Allegheny Mountains to the Forks of the Ohio. This route was followed by Forbes' Army which seized Fort Duquesne in 1758. With the conquest of Canada a few years later, an English-speaking civilization was permanently established in America.

9

The Indian's Way of Life was changed by the Trader's Goods — Exhibit 4A

(page 12)

3A. The Neglected Ohio Becomes a World-Famous River

Historically and geographically the Ohio River is one of the most important rivers in America. It is 987 miles long and is fed by a basin of 203,900 square miles. The river remained unknown for almost 200 years after the discovery of America. The three maps in this case show the emergence of the Ohio River from obscurity to international prominence.

Although the French knew of the Ohio River as early as the 17th century, the Wabash River was their principal access from the Mississippi to the Lakes and Montreal. The British, on the other hand, had little knowledge of or concern for the Ohio River until their first conflicts with the French in 1754. The French found the Ohio River strategically important in supplying Fort Duquesne and the other upper Ohio posts with flour and meat from Illinois, the "bread basket of New France."

By this time the British belatedly realized that the French possession of the Forks of the Ohio blocked off access to the great western country. The Ohio River now became a prize of international importance. Because of its strategic position as a military highway, the development of dependable maps became a critical necessity.

The case contains three maps: *Carte de la Louisiane,* 1685, an anonymous map from the Service Hydrographique in Paris; *Karte von Louisiana,* 1744, an original print from the map by the famous French geographer, Jacques Nicholas Bellin; *A Map of the Ohio Country,* 1752, by John Patten, made from information gained while held captive by the Indians in 1750-51. The original is in the Library of Congress. At first greatest emphasis was placed on the Wabash River, the principal access of the French from Canada to Louisiana. The Allegheny and Ohio were treated as a single river. The Forks of the Ohio were difficult to identify because the Monongahela River, if shown at all, appeared as a minor tributary.

3B. The Lifeline of New France Was Long and Difficult to Maintain

This case contains a decorative map of French possessions, the principal towns and settlements, grazing lands, hunting districts of the fur trade, mines and the like. In mid-18th century France resolved to unite her far-flung American possessions which extended almost 3,000 miles from the St. Lawrence River to the Gulf of Mexico. The routes through the Great Lakes and the Ottawa River had been

11

used since the 17th century. But it now became clear that the Ohio River, the shortest and most navigable route, was destined to form the most vital link between Canada and Louisiana, neither of which was self-supporting in food supply. From the fine farming and grazing lands of the Illinois, then called the "Granary of New France," products were to be shipped north and south and especially to the headwaters of the Ohio River where Fort Duquesne stood as defense against any British effort to sever this lifeline of New France.

4A. The Indian's Life Was Changed by the Trader's Goods

This case contains important artifacts of the periods both before and after the advent of the white man, such as stone implements, clay pots, beads and arrow points as well as trade goods including rifles, metal tomahawks, iron pots, knives, jew's harps and manufactured beads. There is a portrait of Lap-pa-win-soe, a Delaware chief, representative of the 18th century Pennsylvania Indian. His hair is worn long and there is no feathered headdress (see illustration, p. 10).

Before the arrival of Europeans, the Indians of western Pennsylvania followed a way of life that had changed little over several thousand years. The Indian obtained food by farming, hunting, fishing, and gathering seeds, berries and the like. Villages consisted of circular bark huts surrounded by a stockade wall. Tools and clothing were made from wood, stone, clay, and hides.

As tribal society broke down under European influence and domination, native crafts declined and disappeared. The bow and arrow was abandoned for the flintlock musket, clay pots for brass kettles, stone tools for metal ones, and animal skins for English cloth. These new goods were obtained by barter and by alliances that always worked to the disadvantage of the Indian. The deadly effects of liquor and disease played a major role in disrupting and destroying the native communities.

From 1747 to 1753 Logstown (see inset diorama) was the most important local Indian village. Located 18 miles below the Forks of the Ohio it contained some 40 log cabins built for the Indians, mostly by the French. Before Logstown was destroyed by fire in 1754, it provided the setting for important treaties and negotiations.

4B. Kuskuski, Early Delaware Village, Revealed by Archaeology

The several Kuskuski village sites, located near present-day New Castle, were occupied in succession from about 1730 to 1790 by In-

12

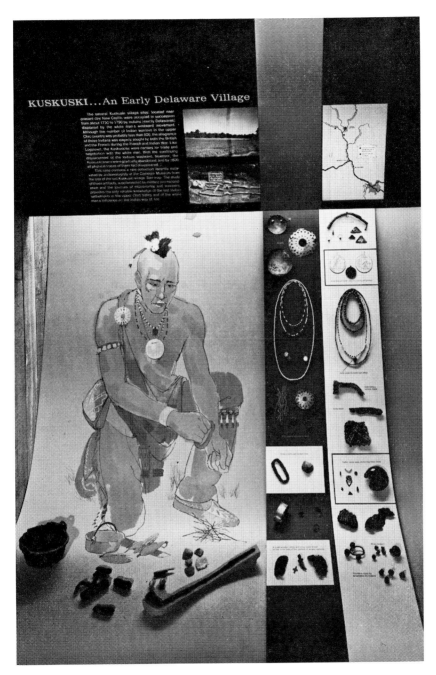

Kuskuski: An Early Delaware Village is revealed by Archaeology — Exhibit 4B

(*page 12*)

13

dians (mainly Delawares) displaced by the white man's westward movement. Although the number of Indian warriors in the upper Ohio country was probably less than 800, the allegiance of those Indians was eagerly sought by both the British and the French during the French and Indian War. Like Logstown, the Kuskuski villages were centers for trade and negotiation with the white man. With the continuing displacement of the Indians westward, however, the Kuskuski towns were gradually abandoned, and by 1800 all physical traces of them had disappeared (see illustration, p. 13).

This case contains a rare collection recently excavated by arch- aeologists of the Carnegie Museum from the site of the last Kuskuski village, shown by a map and a photograph of the actual site. The study of these artifacts, supplemented by military correspondence and the journals of missionaries and travelers, provides the only reliable knowledge of the last Indian settlements in the upper Ohio Valley and of the white man's influence on the Indian way of life.

5. The Céloron Expedition — France Claims the Ohio Valley

Alarmed by growing English trade and influence among Indians of the Upper Ohio where Virginia planned a fort, the Governor of Canada in 1749 sent Captain Céloron de Blainville with 250 French and Indians on a journey shown on the map, warning away traders and seeking Indian allegiance.

At the mouths of six tributaries of the Allegheny and Ohio Rivers, marked on the map by *fleur-de-lis* insignia, Céloron conducted ceremonies in the name of King Louis XV, nailing the royal arms to trees and planting lead plates to claim French ownership of the territory. This ceremony is depicted in a small painting. Finding con- ditions even more grave than expected, the French resolved to occupy the territory and to fortify the Forks of the Ohio.

A copy of the lead plate left by Céloron at the confluence of the Ohio and Kanawha Rivers is exhibited in the case. The original was discovered in 1848 by a boy playing on the banks of the Kanawha and is now owned by the Virginia Historical Society in Richmond, Virginia, through whose courtesy this copy was made. A translation of the text of the plate reads:

"The year 1749, in the reign of Louis XV, King of France, We, Céloron, commandant of a detachment sent by Monsier the

14

The Trader led the Way to the Wilderness — Exhibit 6A

(*page 16*)

15

M[arquis] de La Galissoniere, commander in chief of New France, to restore tranquility in some Indian villages of these districts have buried this plate AT THE MOUTH OF THE RIVER CHINODAHICHETHA THE 18 AUGUST, near the river Ohio, otherwise Beautiful river, as a monument of the renewal of possession which we have taken of the said river Ohio and of all those which fall into it, of all lands on both sides of it as far as the sources of said streams, as enjoyed or ought to be, by the preceding Kings of France and as they have maintained themselves by arms and treaties, especially by those of Ryswick, Utrecht and Aix La Chapelle."

6A. The Trader Led the Way to the Wilderness

The Indian trader was the forerunner of the white man's civilization. For the Indian's furs and skins, he bartered utensils and tools, clothing and trinkets, guns and ammunition and also rum and brandy. These caused profound changes in the native's way of life, making him dependent on the men who sought to take his land. Because of the trader's familiarity with the Indian's life and language, he was often influential in governmental relations with them. The French and British contended bitterly for domination of this trade, not only for its profit but also to bind the Indians to them as allies. This case contains a lifelike model of the trader and his pack train as well as genuine artifacts pertaining to his trade (see illustration, p. 15).

There is an original trader's license, issued by Sir William Johnson, New York Indian agent, and signed by his Western Deputy, George Croghan, at Fort Pitt in 1762 (loaned by the Darlington Library of the University of Pittsburgh).

An original and rare smooth-bore flintlock musket of the 1750-1760 period is displayed. This was the forerunner of the Pennsylvania rifle. The accuracy of fire of the smooth-bore musket was greatly increased by the introduction of spiral grooves or "rifling" which distinguished the Pennsylvania rifle, extensively used by the frontiersmen and often by American militiamen.

After furs had been packed in bales for transportation, they were fastened with official lead seals to prevent tampering en route. Reproductions of French seals recovered from the site of Fort LeBoeuf (modern Waterford, Erie County) are displayed in the case.

Next to his rifle, the frontiersman prized his hatchet and knife. This remarkable kit, preserved from frontier days, is one of the

The Trader's Cabin was the Center of Wilderness Commerce — Exhibit 6B

(*page 18*)

17

prized displays of the museum. Notice the salt horn and horn cup made from animal horn by the resourceful frontiersman.

6B. The Trader's Cabin Was the Center of Wilderness Commerce

Throughout his travels (nearly 5,000 miles) in conducting the Western Pennsylvania Architectural Survey (1932-36), the writer observed hundreds of log houses but found no true frontier log cabin. He therefore resorted to early descriptions and drawings in designing this building and used for its construction the group of experienced lumbermen he employed in the reconstruction of Fort Ligonier. The cabin was first assembled in Westmoreland County then disassembled and re-erected in the museum. The following narration is heard by the visitor as he stands in the cabin (see illustration, p. 17).

"You are standing in a true frontier log cabin, as distinguished from a log house. Notice that the logs are unhewn and still have their bark on. The floor is of beaten earth. Lacking glass and iron, the trader covered his windows with animal skin and made his door and window hinges of wood. His furniture is fashioned with puncheons, or halved logs with the flat sides up.

"In such cabins the traders carried on a profitable commerce with the Indian as early as the 1730's and 40's, before the arrival of the soldier and settler. The trader was a welcome visitor to the Indian whose changed way of life depended on the white man's goods.

"Here you see an Indian bargaining with the trader, offering his deer, beaver, fox and raccoon furs for the blankets he holds. Above all he is interested in obtaining the indispensable musket with a supply of ammunition, as well as steel knives and tomahawks. His squaw will want kettles and both are enamored of vermilion, mirrors, beads, and, among other curious things, a jew's harp. The trader usually ignored the restriction placed by the authorities on the sale of rum or brandy to the Indian as these liquors were a great asset to the trader in his bargaining. Unaccustomed to strong drink, the Indian paid a tragic penalty for his over-indulgence.

"Most trade goods were made in Europe and transmitted to the traders through agents in the eastern cities. Large fortunes were made and lost in this fickle business where credit was loosely enforced. Conflict between the French and English was a constant threat to the owners. The trader led a hard and precarious existence. His intimate knowledge of the Indian was of use to the military and civil authorities and the trader sometimes played a leading role in treaty negotiations."

Fort Presque Isle near the site of present-day Erie — Exhibit 7A

Conjectural Restoration Drawing by Charles M. Stotz

(page 20)

19

7A. The French Invade Western Pennsylvania

The French invasion of what is now western Pennsylvania in 1753 and 1754 achieved its purpose in joining Canada and Louisiana and in forestalling, for a while, the westward expansion of the English colonies. The existence of the newly built Fort Duquesne depended on supplies brought from Canada by the route shown on this panel. This vital lifeline was guarded by the four French forts pictured here by drawings made by the writer from 18th century military plans obtained in European archives.

Fort Niagara, built in 1720 and later enlarged, guarded the Great Lakes route. Goods brought from Montreal were laboriously carried over the steep portage around the Falls and from there by boat to Fort Presque Isle, built in 1753 on the site of modern Erie (see illustration, p. 19). The swampy portage from here to Fort LeBoeuf, also built in 1753 on the site of present-day Waterford (see illustration, p. 21), was almost impassable in wet weather. French Creek, except in low water, carried the canoes and pirogues to Fort Machault, built in 1754 on the site of modern Franklin (see illustration, p. 23). From here the Allegheny River provided an excellent water route to Fort Duquesne at the Forks of the Ohio.

7B. The Army of New France Was Well Equipped

Troops on the frontier were militia forces conscripted from various parishes of Canada. Officers were generally chosen from regiments sent from the mother country. The French, to a far greater extent than the British, made use of Indian allies in military engagements, and it was not uncommon for French officers to lead bands of Indian warriors. Among the many distinguished original artifacts purchased for the museum, this case contains some of the most interesting.

The Charlevoix musket, a type of smooth-bore flintlock musket carried by the French foot soldier, was named for one of the Royal Armories in France where this weapon was made. It was lighter than its British counterpart, the Brown Bess. Both weapons were inferior to the rifles used by some Colonial troops. Also shown is a type of military sword with its original scabbard. It was carried by French officers. Another sword with an attractive shell design on the hilt is characteristic of the period. The shorter sword was better suited for forest warfare.

Fort LeBoeuf at the site of present-day Waterford — Exhibit 7A

Conjectural Restoration Drawing by Charles M. Stotz

(*page 20*)

21

The spontoon, a type of pole-arm or spear, was carried at the head of a company of troops, usually by its sergeant. The spontoon served as a rallying point for troops and as a means of communicating orders over the din of battle to advance or retreat. Officers carried pistols as well as swords. The embossed silver fittings and carved wooden stocks of the pair of matching flintlock pistols made them elegant for their time. Difference in color of cloth and detail of trim distinguished uniforms of various regiments brought from France and also identified rank. Pictures are included of an officer, a non-commissioned officer and a private soldier.

8A. McKee's Rocks Hill Has a Long Record of Human Occupation

None of the countless hills of Pittsburgh carries such a long record of human occupation or such prominence in the annals of the 18th century as the bare whale-shaped eminence that stands on the Ohio River shore just below the mouth of Chartier's Creek. The relief map in the bottom of the case extends from the Point to this hill, known in the early days as Indian Hill or Fort Hill, and later as McKee's Rocks Hill (see illustration, p. 25).

McKee's Rocks Hill was a favorite Indian site from as early as 3000 B.C. The first two layers of the mound which stood at the tip of the hill, now largely quarried away, were placed by the *Adena* or *Moundbuilder* Indians about 600 B.C. The burial ceremony shown in the painting on the panel to the left of the case is based upon arch-aeological knowledge gained in the excavation of this mound and others in the Ohio Valley. A third layer was placed on the mound about the time of Christ by Indians of the *Hopewell* culture, thus making its height 16 feet and its diameter 85 feet. About 1500 A.D. the *Monongahela People* built elsewhere on the hill a village within a circular stockade. Ditches remaining from an Indian fort were described by visitors in 1753.

The first proposal in historic times to use this hill as a site for a fort was made by the Ohio Company of Virginia for whom their agent, George Mercer, made the drawing in 1753, that is displayed on the right panel of the case. Mercer describes the McKee's Rocks site (shown enlarged in the insert) thus: "Where the Company proposes to erect a Town. It is a Plain [now known as "The Bottoms"] about ¾ of a Mile in Length and ½ a Mile in Breadth, bounded on the North by a very high Hill, where the Fort is to be built, on the South-ward and East by Shurtee's [old spelling for Chartier's] Creek, on the

22

Fort Machault at the site of present-day Franklin — Exhibit 7A

Conjectural Restoration Drawing by Charles M. Stotz

(*page 20*)

Eastward and West by the Ohio River which runs around the Hill."

He describes the cliff, from which McKee's Rocks later took its name, thus: ". . . the East End which is inaccessible, being near 100 feet high and large Rocks jutting one over the other to the Top . . ." These cliffs, which once bore the carved initials of soldiers who visited here from Fort Pitt, have been cut back by quarrying operations some 200 feet in modern times. This drawing is reproduced from the original in the Public Record Office in London.

On his expedition to Fort LeBoeuf in 1753, George Washington had been requested by the Ohio Company of Virginia to visit McKee's Rocks and assess the value of this site for the fort and town which the Company proposed to build here. In comparison with the Point at the Forks of the Ohio, which he had examined the day before, Washington reported that the McKee's Rocks site was ". . . greatly inferior, either for Defence or Advantages . . ." In the diorama in the center of the case Washington is being greeted by Shingiss, King of the Delaware settlement here, as he lands at McKee's Rocks. The ancient Indian mound may be seen above.

Largely on the advice of George Washington, the Virginians built Fort Prince George at the Point in 1754, instead of using the "Fort Hill" at McKee's Rocks. After the fall of Fort Duquesne, also built at the Point, the use of this site for the proposed Fort Pitt raised controversy among the British for eight more years. Colonel Hugh Mercer and his engineer reported to Colonel Bouquet in April 1759 that they favored McKee's Rocks as a site for Fort Pitt, as did the fort's designer, Captain Harry Gordon. However, General John Stanwix ordered the fort built at the Point, regardless of the flood hazard, as this site had absolute command of both rivers.

Fort Pitt suffered a disastrous flood in 1762 and Colonel William Eyre reported to General Amherst his amazement the French had not used the McKee's Rocks site ". . . but it's still as Amazing that we repeated the Mistake . . ." However, the die had been cast and the hill at McKee's Rocks was denied this dramatic climax to its nearly 5,000 years of human occupation. It may be added that George Washington was largely responsible for "locating" Pittsburgh.

8B. Washington Carries the Challenge to Fort LeBoeuf

No task in George Washington's long and active career demanded more fortitude and courage than his mission to Fort LeBoeuf, from October 31, 1753, to January 16, 1754. Upon the shoulders of this 21-year-old youth was placed the grave responsibility of confronting

24

McKee's Rocks Hill has a Long Record of Human Occupation — Exhibit 8A

(page 22)

25

seasoned and hostile French officers, face to face, with the first formal challenge to their invasion of territory claimed by Virginia. Though primarily concerned with private land ownership, this mission proved to be an opening maneuver of the French and Indian War, in which the young Washington was soon to become deeply involved.

This journey of more than 600 miles is described by Washington in his *Diary*. ". . . as fatiguing a Journey as it is Possible to conceive, rendered so by excessive bad Weather; From the first Day of December to the 15th there was but one Day but it rained or snowed incessantly; and throughout the whole Journey we met with nothing but one continued Series of cold wet Weather, which occasioned very uncomfortable Lodgings, especially after we had left our Tent, which was some Screen from the Inclemency of it." Added to this was the ever present peril from hostile Indians and from the French who were committed to driving away the English.

The quotations under the six dioramas in the case are taken from *The Journal of Major George Washington,* published in Williamsburg in 1754. The authorship of the contemporary map of the journey, reproduced below the dioramas, is attributed to George Washington himself. The subjects of the dioramas and the quotations from the *Journal* that describe them are as follows:

1. Williamsburg: October 31. "I was commissioned and appointed by the Honourable Robert Dinwiddie, Esq; Governor, etc. of Virginia, to visit and deliver a Letter to the Commandant of the French Forces on the Ohio, and set out on the intended Journey the same day; . . ." At Winchester he "engaged Mr. Gist to pilot us out, and also hired four others as Servitors, . . ." as well as Jacob Vanbraam as his French interpreter.

2. Forks of the Ohio: November 22. ". . . , I spent some Time in viewing the Rivers, and the Land in the Fork, which I think extremely well situated for a Fort, as it has the absolute Command of both Rivers . . . a considerable Bottom of flat, well-timbered Land, . . . very convenient for Building."

3. Logstown: November 25 to 30. Here Washington stopped to confer with the local representatives of the Six Nations and to seek their aid in carrying out his mission. The Seneca chief, Half-King, told of his rebuff by the French officers at LeBoeuf when he had warned them off the land. After aggravating delays the Half-King with three other Indians set off with Washington's party.

4. Fort LeBoeuf: December 11 to 16. En route to LeBoeuf Wash-

26

ington had stopped at Venango (modern Franklin) where he received an abrupt retort from Chabert Joncaire, the French half-breed, "That it was their absolute Design to take Possession of the Ohio, and by God they would do it . . ." At LeBoeuf Washington received a more gracious reception but no less firm reply from the commandant, Legardeur de St. Pierre, who disdained Dinwiddie's summons to retire and stated that ". . . the country belonged to them."

5. Connoquenessing Creek: December 27. On the return from Venango when Washington and Gist set out alone on foot ". . . we fell in with a Party of French Indians, who had laid in Wait for us; one of them fired at Mr. Gist or me, not 15 steps, but fortunately missed."

6. Allegheny River Crossing: December 29. Finding the river running with ice, they improvised a raft. Halfway over, the raft jammed in the ice and began to sink. In trying to free the raft with his pole, Washington was thrown into ten feet of water. He regained the raft but, being enable to make either shore, decided ". . . , as we were near an Island [Wainwright's Island, since dredged away], to quit our Raft and make to it." The next morning they reached the mainland on new ice.

9. The French Occupied the Forks of the Ohio from 1754 to 1758

This diorama shows the occupation of the Point in April of 1754. The flotilla of 60 bateaux and 300 canoes had just arrived from Canada by way of the Allegheny River. The force of 500 French and Indians landed without resistance, set up two of their 18 cannon, and demanded the surrender of the little English garrison of 41 workmen and soldiers. After a brief parley the French graciously agreed to permit the men to leave with their tools and arms. This little fort which consisted of nothing more than a log house in which to store Indian trade goods surrounded by a stockade wall bore the impressive name of Fort Prince George. It had been built on order of the Ohio Company, a group of Virginia gentlemen and land speculators who had hoped to establish possession of the Forks of the Ohio before the French arrived. The French proceeded to build Fort Duquesne and to maintain control of the Ohio Valley until 1758.

10A. The French and Indian War Began on Chestnut Ridge

The drawing on this panel shows a portion of Chestnut Ridge and the path which extended from Fort Necessity across the Ridge

27

Washington Surrenders to the French at Fort Necessity — Exhibit 10C

(*page 29*)

28

to the glen where the skirmish took place between George Washington's forces and those of Jumonville. The panel also contains descriptions of the Jumonville Affair and the Surrender of Fort Necessity.

Both the French and the British were determined to possess the Forks of the Ohio. War was not declared until 1756, but the first blood was shed in 1754.

10B. Washington Wins His First Battle

This diorama shows the rocky ravine near Chestnut Ridge where an encampment of French soldiers from Fort Duquesne was surprised at daybreak on May 27, 1754, by a small Colonial force under George Washington. In this battle, Washington's first, ten Frenchmen were killed, including their leader, Coulon de Jumonville. The French called this an unprovoked act of war in time of peace and labeled Washington an assassin. The British countered that the French had concealed themselves with intent to ambush their camp. About a month later, Coulon de Villiers, brother of Jumonville, set out from Fort Duquesne to avenge his brother's "murder."

10C. Washington Surrenders to the French at Fort Necessity

The diorama on the left shows the little stockaded enclosure, aptly named Fort Necessity, where Washington, with 360 Colonials, resisted the attack of 900 French and Indians. Rain fell steadily through the two-day battle, filling the defensive ditches around the fort. With both sides short of ammunition, the French, faced with the defection of their Indian allies, and the British, getting the worst of it, a parley was held on July 4. The English capitulated with the honors of war. Having lost almost all of their horses and oxen, supplies and wounded had to be carried on foot (see illustration, p. 28). The French could not completely restrain their Indian allies who feigned attack, causing panic among the retreating troops. After destroying the fort, and any other vestiges of English settlement that could be found, the French returned to the stronghold of their new inland empire, Fort Duquesne.

11A. Plans of Fort Duquesne Were Recorded by the British

Fort Duquesne, like most of the frontier forts, was square in plan with bastions projecting from each corner. The purpose of the

29

bastion was to provide a flanking fire in front of the neighboring bastions and along the curtain wall connecting them. In short, there was no cover for an attacker.

The 18th century army engineer had rule-of-thumb guidelines for laying out a fort in the field. Fort Duquesne conforms to one such formula, as illustrated by a model of the north wall.

This case contains two famous contemporary plans of Fort Duquesne and a model explaining the nature of an 18th century frontier fort.

The drawing at the top of the case shows Fort Duquesne and its auxiliary fort on the banks of the Allegheny River as they appeared to Forbes' troops. The French had burned, mined and demolished these structures as completely as possible before leaving. The absence of buildings from the drawing would indicate that they had been effectually destroyed. This drawing, reproduced from the original in the Map Room of the British Museum, was drawn by a leading military engineer with the British Army, J. C. Pleydell. He likewise made drawings of Fort Ligonier and Fort Bedford which are preserved in the Royal Library at Windsor Castle.

The drawing at the bottom of the case attracted worldwide attention in the 18th century when it was published with the account of the remarkable exploits of its author, Major Robert Stobo. Stobo was a hostage given the French after the battle of Fort Necessity. He made this drawing secretly while confined in Fort Duquesne. On the back of the drawing he wrote a full description of the fort and its armament. This drawing was smuggled to Virginia by a friendly Indian. When the same drawing was retrieved from the effects of General Edward Braddock after his defeat in 1755, Stobo was revealed as a spy and tried for his life. The drawing and letter were used in evidence, as the notations and signatures in French on the drawing indicate. The information thus supplied was substantially correct but never used. Stobo escaped to England and later returned to America. The original is in the Canadian Archives in Ottawa. As the original drawing is almost illegible, a modern transcription of the drawing and its lettering is also displayed.

11B. Fort Duquesne Was Small and Poorly Built

The two plans displayed in this case provide the most complete and authentic information about the design and construction of Fort Duquesne. They were drawn by French military engineers while those in case 11A were made by Englishmen.

Upon learning early in 1755 that the British were assembling an army in Virginia for an attack on Fort Duquesne, the commandant, Sieur de Contrecoeur, recognized the immediate necessity of repairing and strengthening Fort Duquesne which had been badly damaged by floods. He therefore summoned the one man in Canada experienced in this field, Lieutenant Chaussegros de Léry, who prepared this plan and report in April of 1755. De Léry warned that the fort, because of its "many capital defects," could not be defended before an army and that the French "must engage the enemy before the formation of a siege." This is exactly the way it happened in July of 1755. The French and Indians under Captain Beaujeu sallied from Fort Duquesne and routed Braddock's Army when only three miles from the Point, thus avoiding the almost certain destruction of the little French fort.

The other plan is unsigned. It is the only existing contemporary drawing of Fort Duquesne which provides a complete plan of the fort and a legend giving the use of all the buildings in it. The original of this drawing is in the Bibliotheque Nationale in Paris. The horizontal log walls and stockade walls are clearly shown, as are the cannon platforms and even the bunks in the barracks. The "platform for barbette," shown in the southeast bastion, was an elevated platform which enabled the cannon to fire over the parapet. All the other cannon fired through embrasures or openings in the parapet (see illustration, p. 32).

Such frontier forts built of earth and timber were subject to rapid deterioration from erosion, rust and rot and required continuous maintenance or replacement. They were usually built in haste when the enemy was near at hand and abandoned when the emergency had passed.

The demi-lunes, or V-shaped islands on the eastern and southern sides of the fort, contain buildings instead of the usual ramparts, indicating the drastic need for space in this little fort.

On the platform between the two maps there are two models, one showing the method of constructing a stockade wall and the other the building of a horizontal log wall. These models are supplemented by two cut-away drawings.

The eastern and southern sides of the fort were built of a double wall of horizontal logs about 10 feet apart connected by bonding logs. This structure formed a sort of basketwork which was filled with earth and stones. This type of construction is shown in the cut-away

31

PLAN du Fort Duquesne.

A. Logement du Commandant.
B. Chambre du Garde des Magasins.
C. Petit magasin de détail.
D. Distribution.
E. Logement des Cadets.
F. Prison.
G. Chambres pour les Officiers et Aumonier.
H. Les Casernes.
I. La forge.
K. La Boulangerie.

L. Les Latrines.
M. Magasin aux Poudres.
N. Plattes-formes.
O. Platteforme a Barbe.
P. Pont Levis.
Q. Pont Dormant.
R. Logement de l'In...
S. Logement des Chi...
T. Hôpital.
V. Magasin.

Echelle de 30.Toises.

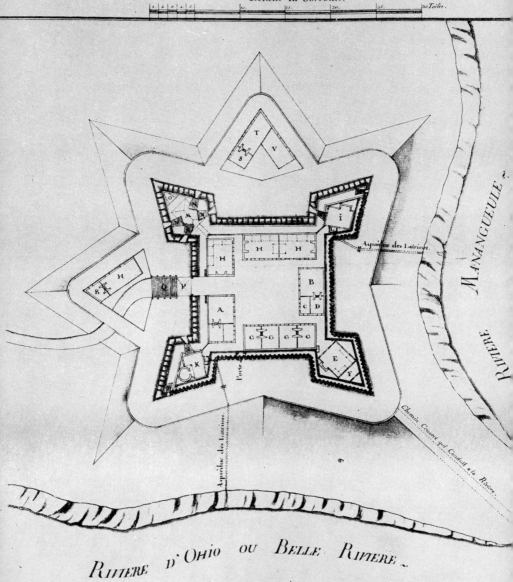

Aqueduc des Latrines.

RIVIERE MANANGUEULE.

Chemin Couvert qui Conduit a la Rivière.

Aqueduc des Latrines.

Porte.

RIVIERE D'OHIO OU BELLE RIVIERE.

drawing and in the model below. Such a rampart provided substantial resistance to artillery fire. To build this kind of wall required a great deal of time and material. Therefore it was used only on the sides of the fort most subject to attack. In the case of Fort Duquesne these were the sides facing the land.

The sides of Fort Duquesne that faced the river were palisade walls, composed of vertical logs or pickets, a foot thick and 12 feet high, with an elevated firing platform. The sectional drawing and model show the nature and method of constructing a palisade wall.

11C. Fort Duquesne Is Re-created by a Model

From April of 1754 until November of 1758 France held undisputed control of the land west of the mountains. Fort Duquesne and its little French village, commanding the headwaters of the Ohio, secured the river route uniting Canada and Louisiana.

The first fort, constructed of earthwork and timber between 1754 and 1756, was much too small to house the garrison and its munitions and supplies. The "Second Fort," built between 1757 and 1758, was a simple stockaded enclosure (see illustration, p. 35).

The French recognized the weakness and inadequacy of the fort but were unable to take any corrective measures before the war was over.

The research, preparation of scale drawings and the construction of this model required more time and effort than any other exhibit in the Museum. Research began in 1955 with the fortunate discovery in the Bibliotheque Nationale in Paris of the only definitive plan of Fort Duquesne, without which an authentic model could not have been built. However, this drawing gave only the plan layout and use of the various buildings and nothing of their appearance above ground, which had to be worked out from fragmentary references in French and British military archives, through military correspondence and occasional sketches of other forts. Visits were therefore made to the principal archives and fort sites in North America. These supplementary sources shed some light on the "Second Fort" along the Allegheny River, outbuildings and work areas, topography, landing sites, gardens and the extensive Indian Camp, as well as the nature of the French bateaux, pirogues, rafts and flatboats and the cargo they carried. In making the model drawings at a scale of one inch equals twenty feet, the elements of conjecture were supplied by a general

RT DUQUESNE
om a drawing in the Bibliotheque Nationale, Paris, PoC13922

knowledge of the building methods and living conditions common to most French forts. The scope of this account is too limited to provide detailed descriptions of the fort which is presented in *Drums in the Forest* and will be more fully presented in a forthcoming work by the writer. The actual fabrication of the model is a masterpiece of craftsmanship by Harold and Raymond Yoest of Holiday Displays, the contractor for the exhibits.

12A. *Braddock's Tragic Defeat Made News in Europe*

This diorama shows a relief map of the battle site with an overlay explaining the successive actions in the engagement. Six original prints of the Orme engravings, described below, are mounted on the case wall.

The total defeat of Braddock's well-equipped army of 1,469 men by 200 French soldiers and 400 Indians on July 9, 1755, made sensational news in Europe. This incredible disaster was all the more tragic because Braddock, after cutting 125 miles of military roads through densely wooded mountainous country, lost everything when only six miles from Fort Duquesne. How could this have happened? Who was responsible? At the time the blame was largely placed on Braddock, who lost his life in the battle. Later research has restored much of his tarnished reputation.

The army twice crossed the Monongahela River to avoid the danger of ambush in the deep Turtle Creek Valley. The second crossing was accomplished by mid-afternoon. When only a half mile from the river Braddock's advance party, which was moving along a 12-foot road in narrow formation, surprised the approaching French forces. The French forces are clearly designated on Plan V. This plan was used in making the diagrammatic model (within the case) showing the terrain of the battle site and the formation of the opposing forces as they met.

The British immediately formed and delivered a heavy fire, killing Captain Daniel Beaujeu, the commander. Captain Jean Dumas took his place and promptly deployed his men as so many ants surrounding a giant caterpillar. The Indians took cover behind trees and in ravines and also seized the commanding hill to the right which the British had foolishly neglected to occupy. This tactical error was followed by another. The advance party was ordered to retreat but was prevented from doing so by the advancing vanguard which in turn could not fall back because of the baggage train behind it which had

not halted as it was ordered to do. In the resulting confusion all semblance of discipline and order was lost.

After repeated efforts to rally his troops, in which Braddock played a conspicuous and brave part until he was mortally wounded, the army fled in panic, leaving cannon, baggage, cattle, and the wounded for the Indians to ravage. Critics praised George Washington for his heroic role in the battle. The most severe losses were suffered by Washington's Virginian troops. In their location as flanking scouts they received the fire not only of the outlying Indians but also the British regulars in the center. The site of the battle lay in present-day Braddock and is largely covered by the Edgar Thomson Works of the United States Steel Corporation.

Descriptions of the battle action and also sketches of the site and disposition of the troops have been left for us by a few participants, including Captain Robert Orme, aide-de-camp to General Edward Braddock. Original engravings made from the Orme sketches are displayed in this case. The titles of these engravings and descriptions beneath them provide authentic information of the march from Will's Creek and the engagement itself.

The Orme drawings show the detailed disposition of the troops and the deployment of the advance party to guard against surprise while the road was being cut. By road is meant a path through the forest just wide enough to admit wagons and wheeled artillery. Rock outcrops and trees were removed with great difficulty and mountain grades posed tremendous problems. The drawing of the army encampments en route is most interesting. On George Washington's advice General Braddock advanced from his last encampment with about 1200 of the best troops and a minimum of artillery and baggage, the best remaining with Colonel Dunbar. A detailed review of the Orme plans is not feasible in this review.

12B. Braddock's Retreat Became a Disorganized Flight

This diorama shows the retreat across the Monongahela near the mouth of Turtle Creek. After three agonizing hours of devastating fire by the French and Indians from their forest cover, the British troops lost all semblance of discipline. General Braddock gave up any hope of reorganizing his men and ordered a retreat, at which point he was mortally wounded. Washington, and the few remaining officers who had not been killed, tried to control the troops but they fled in

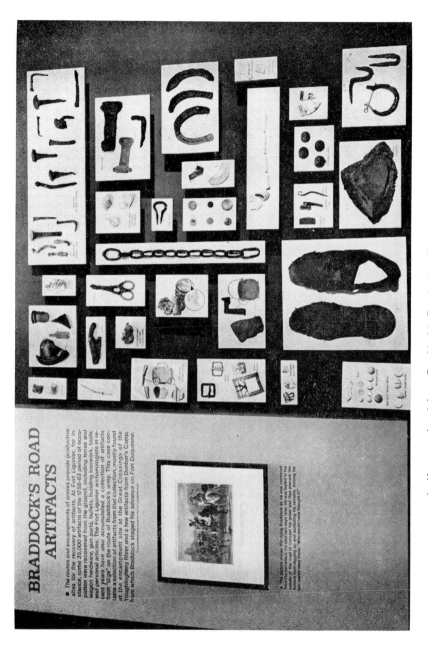

Artifacts retrieved from Braddock's Road tell a Story — Exhibit 12C

(*page 38*)

37

panic across the Monongahela River, leaving the wounded and the baggage to the mercy of the Indians.

12C. Artifacts Retrieved from Braddock's Road Tell a Story

The routes and encampments of armies provide productive sites for the recovery of artifacts. At Fort Ligonier, for instance, some 35,000 artifacts of the 1758-63 period of occupation were recovered from the grounding including horse and wagon hardware, gun parts, bullets, building ironwork, tools, and personal articles. The Fort Ligonier archaeologists in recent years have also accumulated a collection of artifacts from "digs" on the route of Braddock's army. This case contains a selection of artifacts from that collection, mostly found at the encampment site at the Great Crossings of the Youghiogheny River and a few artifacts from Dunbar's Camp, from which Braddock staged his advance on Fort Duquesne. These artifacts have been loaned by the Fort Ligonier Museum. Among these 200-year-old objects, note the well preserved leather shoes, shell fragment, building hardware, uniform buttons and the jew's harp, a popular trade item with the Indians (see illustration, page 37).

The picture shows the dying Braddock as he was conveyed from the battlefield. He died two days later. He was buried in the middle of the road to conceal his grave and thus prevent the Indians from digging up and mutilating his remains. Among his last words were these: "Who would have thought it?"

13A. A Reign of Terror Gripped the Border from 1755 to 1758

The defeat of Braddock left the frontier open and defenseless. For the next three years a nightmare of death and destruction was inflicted on the border, even to the settlements east of the mountains. The Indians were incited and led by French soldiers from Fort Duquesne which Colonel Bouquet described as ". . . that nest of Pirates which has so long harboured the murderers and destructors of our poor People."

The harrowing details of the diorama entitled *Indian Raid* (see illustration, p. 39) are taken from border annals of the time. The husband is struck down at the plow by one Indian while another attacks his wife and children and a third Indian moves to set fire to the cabin. In spite of these raids and in defiance of a royal decree forbidding settlement beyond the mountains, the settlers doggedly perse-

The Indian swore Vengeance on the Settler who occupied his Land — Exhibit 13A

(*page 38*)

vered in their determination to occupy the frontier lands of the Indian. The Indian by this time recognized the settler as a greater menace than the European armed forces whose plans of conquest were not so obvious to the Indian.

13B. 1758 Was the Year of Victory

After four years of humiliating defeats and harrowing border raids by the French and Indians, the British in 1758 undertook a massive four-pronged campaign under General James Abercromby to subdue the Indians and to drive the French from America. Although Abercromby himself was unsuccessful in his attempt to take Fort Carillon (Ticonderoga), the other three expeditions achieved their objectives as follows.

General Jeffery Amherst seized the great citadel of Louisbourg which guarded access to Canada by way of the St. Lawrence River.

Captain John Bradstreet captured Fort Frontenac which controlled the entrance to the Great Lakes. He destroyed the French lakes fleet as well as extensive stores largely destined for Fort Duquesne.

General John Forbes assembled an army of some 6,000 men at Raystown (Fort Bedford). After arduous travel over crude mountain roads by way of Fort Ligonier he occupied the ruins of Fort Duquesne November 25, 1758.

Thus the British gained control of the headwaters of the Ohio River where they built their most elaborate stronghold in America, Fort Pitt. With the fall of Fort Niagara and Quebec in 1759 the French in Canada were annihilated and Anglo-Saxon civilization was established from the Atlantic Ocean to the Mississippi River.

13C. The French Are Finally Driven from the Forks of the Ohio

This informative exhibit of the Forbes Campaign is illustrated by five successive color drawings of the important episodes of the march, set against a painted map of the route from Fort Bedford to the Forks of the Ohio. These masterly water-color drawings by Nat Youngblood were based on material assembled by the writer from the *Papers of Colonel Henry Bouquet* and the Crown Collection of American Maps in the British Museum.

Victory for the British came in 1758. In November, General John Forbes seized Fort Duquesne and drove the French from the Ohio Valley forever. To accomplish this task, the army had to make its own road through one hundred miles of forests and mountains. (*View of Troops Assembling at Fort Bedford.*) During the summer of 1758 Forbes assembled at Fort Bedford an army of 2,000 British regulars (see illustration, p. 42). There were also 4,000 provincial troops who were poorly trained and badly equipped. The incomparable Colonel Henry Bouquet assumed immediate command under Forbes who was fatally ill and had to be carried by litter most of the way.

The troops moved westward in late August. (*Army Train Ascending Mountain Road.*) The mountain grades were steep and rough and subject to slides of earth and rock. Men and horses, weakened by overwork, exposure and poor food, were reduced to exhaustion. Few expeditions in frontier history required more sustained effort and physical hardship.

Fortified posts were built at strategic locations for storage of supplies and to provide refuge, if needed. (*Construction of Fort Ligonier.*) The most important of these strongholds was Fort Ligonier, halfway to Fort Duquesne. This typical wilderness fort was made of the earth, stone and timber that lay about it. Here the army was gradually assembled after crossing the mountains from Fort Bedford.

On September 9, Major James Grant with 800 men, mostly Highlanders, suffered a humiliating defeat. He was ordered to reconnoiter Fort Duquesne and to take a few prisoners, but to avoid open conflict. However, when Grant came within sight of the fort without being detected by the French, he became over-confident and rashly decided to attack. After carefully arranging his troops on the densely wooded hillside, the advance was signaled by the drummers beating reveille. Whereupon the French and Indians swarmed from their fort in overwhelming numbers, surrounded the British, and inflicted a loss of 270, including prisoners, as portrayed on the cover of this book. The general area of the engagement is marked by present-day Grant Street, named for the reckless Scot. (*Grant's Engagement.*)

The Indians celebrated their victory by returning to their homes where they could enjoy their loot. Although the defection of Indian allies from the French army was a very real gain for the British in this unfortunate affair, the defeat of Grant was disheartening. Forbes called a staff meeting on November 11 when it was decided to stay the winter at Fort Ligonier. This decision was reversed a few days later, however, when the true weakness of Fort Duquesne and its garrison was discovered. Forbes thereupon ordered the advance, arriving at Fort Duquesne on November 25. (*Forbes at Fort Duquesne.*)

General Forbes assembled his Troops at Fort Bedford — Exhibit 13C

(*page 41*)

The French had been prepared to abandon their wooden fort if they could not defeat the British before they reached the Forks of the Ohio. In this they had been successful against Braddock three years earlier. Using the same strategy, the French and Indians had attacked Fort Ligonier on October 12 and 13 but had been driven off by the British without decisive effect. Now, with the British but one day's march away, they knew their cause to be hopeless. Having destroyed Fort Duquesne with fire and explosives, the French left by the rivers, never to return.

On his arrival Forbes described Fort Duquesne as a scene of "total desolation and wreckage." A letter from General John Forbes to Prime Minister William Pitt bore the significant heading, "Pittsbourgh, November 27th, 1758." Thus was Pittsburgh christened. Forbes wrote: "Sir, I do myself the Honour of acquainting you that it has pleased God to crown His Majesty's Arms with Success over all His Enemies upon the Ohio . . . I have used the Freedom of giving your name to Fort Duquesne . . ." Forbes continued with the prediction that this newly-won territory "will soon be the richest and most fertile of any posses^t by the British in N^o America." Fort Pitt itself was not officially named until November of 1759 when General John Stanwix wrote William Pitt: "I have given this Fort your Name as my predecessor did the Town . . ." Within two years the completed Fort Pitt, largest fortification of Great Britain in America, stood as the symbol of British sovereignty over the land beyond the mountains.

13D. Forbes' Army Included Both Regular and Provincial Troops
Composition of the Army of General John Forbes — 1758

77th Regiment of Highlanders . . .	1,300
Colonel Archibald Montgomery	
Major James Grant	
60th Regiment of Royal Americans . .	350
Colonel Henry Bouquet	
Royal Artillery	40
Pennsylvania Regiment	2,700
1st Battalion — Colonel John Armstrong	
2nd Battalion — Colonel James Burd	
3rd Battalion — Colonel Hugh Mercer	
Virginia Regiments	1,600

1st — Colonel George Washington
2nd — Colonel William Byrd III

Maryland Detachment		300
North Carolina Detachment		200
Lower Counties (Delaware) Detachment	.	300
Total . .		6,790

13E. Forbes Ordered a Day of Thanksgiving for Their Victory

This diorama shows the army gathered before the ruins of Fort Duquesne, with the ailing General sitting in the foreground. The Monongahela River is seen in the background.

November 26, 1758, "was observed, by the General's Orders, as a Day of publick Thanksgiving to Almighty God for our Success; . . ." The Reverend Charles Clinton Beatty, chaplain of the Pennsylvania Regiment, was "appointed to preach a Thanksgiving Sermon for the remarkable Superiority of His Majesty's Arms." Bouquet, in a letter of November 25, described the pitiful condition of the army, a far cry from the manner in which it is usually depicted: "The men are greatly reduced, deficient of every necessary, half naked, without shoes, and without means of getting any. We have neither Tents nor Bagage, but are in good spirits . . ."

14A. The Blockhouse, Built in 1764, Miraculously Survives Today

The three earthen ramparts on the western or downstream sides of Fort Pitt were partially washed away by the record floods of 1762 and 1763. To protect these damaged ramparts Colonel Henry Bouquet built three redoubts at a little distance from the fort. One of these redoubts, finished in 1764, is the building we now know as the Blockhouse. Two redoubts added later on the Monongahela and Allegheny River banks made a total of five, as shown on the plan of the fort area.

The Blockhouse stands on its original site and elevation. It is the oldest building of authenticated date west of the mountains. It miraculously survived 130 years of varied occupancy, mutilation, and neglect until 1894 when it was presented by Mrs. Mary Elizabeth Schenley to the Daughters of the American Revolution of Allegheny County, who restored the building and made it a public monument. The Blockhouse and the foundations of the Music Bastion remain the only vestiges of the elaborate military defenses of the British Empire that once existed at the Point.

THE BLOCKHOUSE

■ The three earthen ramparts on the western or down stream sides of Fort Pitt were partially washed away by the record floods of 1762 and 1763. To protect these damaged ramparts Colonel Henry Bouquet built three redoubts at a little distance from the fort. One of these redoubts finished in 1764 is the building we now know as The Blockhouse. Two redoubts added later on the Monongahela and Allegheny river banks made a total of five, of which only the Blockhouse remains today.

The Blockhouse stands on its original site and elevation. It is the oldest building of authenticated date west of the mountains. It miraculously survived 130 years of varied occupancy, mutilation, and neglect until 1894 when it was presented by Mrs. Mary Elizabeth Schenley to the Daughters of the American Revolution of Allegheny County, who restored the building and made it a public monument. The Blockhouse and the foundations of the Music Bastion remain the only vestiges of the elaborate military defenses that once existed at The Point.

OLD SHORE LINE

The Blockhouse, an authentic and priceless Heirloom of Fort Pitt — Exhibit 14A

(page 44)

45

OR

OHIO

RIVER

FORT PITT

MONONGE

B. O

SECTION through A.B.C.

Scale for the Profil 10 Feet to an Inch

Scale for the Plan 100 Feet to an Inch

EXPLANATION.

The Blockhouse model (see illustration, p. 45) has been cut away to show its construction and to reveal the shape of the "loop-holes" through which soldiers could fire on two levels from all five sides of the building. These redoubts protected the garrison from sniper fire of the Indians which had proved to be a serious hazard in Pontiac's War of 1763.

The photographs show additions and alterations made to the Blockhouse while it was used as a residence. For many years the building was occupied by families of means and importance. Neville B. Craig, Pittsburgh's first historian, was born here in 1787. Jean Barbeau, the distinguished French engineer who published a plan of Pittsburgh in 1830, lived in the Blockhouse in 1831. But for the next half-century the little building, much neglected, was hemmed in by slum dwellings, warehouses and freight yards.

14B. Fort Pitt Was the Most Elaborate British Fort in America

The drawing at the left of the case is the most reliable and informative plan of Fort Pitt (see illustration, p. 46). It is reproduced from the original in the Public Record Office in London which was made from surveys by Lt. Elias Meyer, an engineer in the Royal American Regiment at Fort Pitt. Meyer used surveying instruments similar to those displayed in the case and as shown by the 18th century engraving (from the British Museum) of two surveyors, one sighting through his instrument and the other pushing a wheel by which distances were measured.

Meyer's plan was made in 1761 when the fort was nearing completion. All buildings are named and locations shown for stone quarries, lime and brick kilns, coal pits, and roads. Except for the section through the fort structure, no drawings exist that show the character of the buildings, bridges and other fort structures. This plan of the fort and layout of the King's Gardens was used in the preparation of the fort model displayed in the William Pitt Memorial Hall.

The topographical survey, also by Meyer, was a remarkable project for its time. The entire area around the Forks of the Ohio is clearly shown. Of special interest is the location of the Saw Mill, from which Saw Mill Run Boulevard was named.

As an aid in understanding common fort terms, a drawing of a typical section through an 18th century fortification shows the various parts of the rampart, ditch and glacis, as well as the casemates. The terms are mostly of French origin as they were the masters of the art of war. Most of the field manuals carried by English engineers were based upon handbooks prepared by the French military experts.

14C. Fort Pitt Was Built to Last Forever

Fort Pitt, the mightiest fortress built by the British in America, was designed to withstand the assault of an army and its artillery. However, it was never attacked by an enemy more formidable than unorganized bands of Indians with their arrows and muskets. The effort and money wasted in building this elaborate defense has since aroused much speculation, especially when we consider that the fort construction was just getting under way when French power in America was virtually doomed by the loss of Fort Niagara in July and of Quebec in September of 1759. However valid these examples of hindsight may be, the fact remains that in 1758 William Pitt ordered the construction of a fort strong enough to maintain "the undisputed possession of the Ohio," to protect the colonies from incursions and to establish control of the Indians.

The masonry walls on the eastern faces of Fort Pitt were so durably built that all of the stone footings and some of the lower portions of the brick walls not removed by modern building operations remain in place today, about eight feet underground. A portion of these walls has been permanently exposed to view near the entrance to the park where the visitor may examine at close range the original stone footings and partially-restored brick walls of the Music Bastion (see illustration, p. 93). While one sees here only the lower four feet of the original fort walls, a full-height reconstructed section of the masonry ramparts may be seen just to the right of the entrance to the Fort Pitt Museum.

The lower illustration in the case, based on early records, shows the masonry ramparts under construction (see illustration, p. 49). The ramparts were built of stone with brick facing, 15 feet high, $7\frac{1}{2}$ feet thick at the base and 5 feet thick at the top and surmounted by a stone cap. The external corners of the masonry bastions were edged with stones, known as "quoins." The walls as built conform precisely to the measurements given on the 18th century Meyer drawing, of which a reproduction is shown in this case.

The upper illustration shows the method of building a sod wall. This type of wall was used on the three western ramparts of the fort.

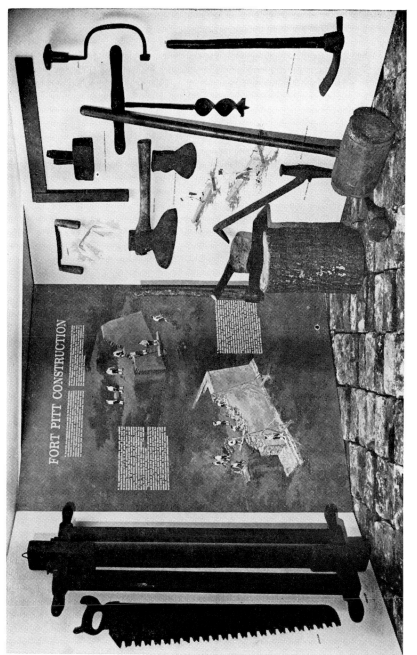

Fort Pitt was built to Maintain "undisputed possession of the Ohio" — Exhibit 14C

(page 48)

49

The 18th century military manuals give explicit directions for sodding an earthen fort wall. Sods were cut to an average size of 3"x12"x18" and laid like brick, alternating headers and stretchers, as shown in the illustration to the right. The green side of the sod was laid downward. To further secure the sods in place, wooden pickets were driven through them at intervals. Colonel Eyre, when he examined Fort Pitt after the disastrous flood of 1762, maintained that much damage resulted from the fact that "in laying the sod they neglected to drive into each 4 or 5 pickets of dry thin wood . . . ." The sod walls required mowing at least twice a year.

The inhabitants were prohibited from allowing animals and fowls to graze on the grass banks or even to dig for worms there! The effects of heavy rain and frost required constant repair. Had it not been for the brick walls on the eastern side, which took the force of the flood currents, the entire fort would have been ruined in the record high water of 1762 and 1763. As it was, the unprotected Ohio Bastion, which projected beyond the brick ramparts, was largely carried away and never entirely replaced.

The implements and tools displayed in this case are of the character of those used in the construction of the fort. They were loaned by the Pennsylvania Farm Museum from their collection of early 19th century tools. The bottom of the case is paved with original bricks from the masonry walls of Fort Pitt. They were recovered by archaeological excavation of the site.

14D. Archaeological Digs Revealed Fort Walls but Few Artifacts

Sub-soil investigations conducted in 1941, 1953, 1958-59 and 1964 have yielded few artifacts of the period of fort occupation, largely because of the disturbance of the original site by periodic flooding and the grading of the land by cutting and filling. The removal of great quantities of earth and portions of the fort wall itself occurred during the construction of the many modern buildings and the freight yards that occupied the fort site.

However, the archaeologists were rewarded by finding in many places remnants of the original stone footings as well as lengths of the lower portions of the brick wall, eight to ten brick courses in height, with the eight-foot-thick rubble stone backing intact. Especially important was the uncovering of the southern point of the Flag Bastion and the northern point of the Music Bastion which established the

The Artillery Casemate, one of ten Casemates within the Ramparts — Exhibit 15A

(*page 53*)

51

terminations of the masonry front of the fort and the beginning of the earth ramparts of which the three western bastions and their curtain walls were built.

The plotting of the various segments of original masonry wall foundations on the modern street grid provided a precise outline of Fort Pitt in its original location. This outline was found to agree almost precisely with the layout of Fort Pitt shown in drawings prepared in 1761 by the military engineers Lt. Elias Meyer and Bernard Ratzer whose plans are preserved in the Public Record Office and British Museum in London. These drawings likewise contain wall sections showing the size and construction of the rampart walls which were found to have been faithfully carried out.

The above story is told by spoken narrative and still-pictures in the sequence projector which comprises Exhibit 14D.

14E. Fort Pitt Was Served by Twenty-Nine Commandants

This list is as complete and dependable as can be managed from available data. Overlapping or duplication of dates occurred when other officers relieved the commandant while he was on leave or on campaign. Properly speaking, General John Stanwix was the first commandant of Fort Pitt, which he officially named in November 1759. Before that time the place was known only as Pittsburgh. Late records are vague and incomplete. Only a small garrison was maintained at Fort Pitt after 1786, and the only known names of officers in charge after that date are Lieutenant Matthew Ernest and Major Isaac Craig.

General John Forbes	1758
Colonel Henry Bouquet	1759, 1760-1762, 1763-1764
Colonel Hugh Mercer	1759
General John Stanwix	1759-1760
Major John Tulleken	1760
Captain Richard Mather	1760
General Robert Monckton	1760
Lieutenant Colonel John St. Clair	1760
Captain Thomas Barnsley	1760
Captain Simeon Ecuyer	1762-1763
Captain William Grant	1764
Captain David Hay	1764
Captain William Murray	1764-1767
Captain Charles Edmonstone	1767-1772

Colonel John Reed	1768
Major Isaac Hamilton	1771-1772
Captain John Connolly	1774
Major John Nevill	1775
Major Robert Campbell	1776
General Edward Hand	1777-1778
General Lachlan McIntosh	1778-1779
Colonel John Gibson	1778-1779, 1781
Colonel Daniel Brodhead	1779-1781
Colonel Stephen Bayard	1781-1783
General William Irvine	1781-1783
Captain John Finley	1783
Major Joseph Marbury	1783-1784
Captain David Lucket	1785
Captain John Armstrong	1786

15A. The Artillery Casemate Served a Vital Function in Defense

This exhibit (see illustration, p. 51) is a full-sized portion of an underground casemate used by the artillery officers in the conversion of bulk army supplies to finished ammunition such as flannel cartridges, fuzes, case shot, grape shot, wads, grenades, shells and the like, as well as to repair muskets and heavy armament. These rooms were built, as were all casemates, with walls of heavy timbers which were doubled on the roof to support the weight of some four feet of earth above them. This served as protection against the most-feared enemy fire — the siege mortar. Great care was taken in these rooms to avoid sparks or contact with flame that might cause an explosion. The disposition of the casemates is shown by diagram in Exhibit 15B.

15B. There Were Nearly 500 Feet of Underground Casemates

There were 12 casemates under the ramparts of the fort, each about 20 feet in width. Their total length was 475 feet. In addition to the two artillery laboratory casemates there were two for the storage of powder, others for storage of supplies and provisions of all kinds, especially salted meat packed in barrels. The actual salting itself was done in the casemates.

The records reveal that, as conditions changed, the casemates were converted to different uses and also suffered greatly from flooding and the inevitable deterioration natural to earthwork and underground timber structures.

Soldiers had comfortable Accommodations in the Barracks of the Fort — Exhibit 17

(*page 55*)

54

16. Loading and Firing the Flintlock Musket Required Dexterity

This sequence projector explains by voice and still-pictures the successive steps in loading and firing a flintlock musket of the period.

17. Fort Pitt Provided Comfortable Barracks for Its Soldiers

This is a portion of a typical room in the soldiers' barracks (see illustration, p. 54). The men slept in double-decked wooden bunks, four-by-six feet in size, and each accommodating two men. The bottoms of the bunks were formed of wide boards covered with straw and sloping slightly toward the foot. Each room had a fireplace and was well lighted by windows with glazed sash. There were three two-story barracks for the soldiers, each about 170 feet long by 20 feet wide, two of frame and one of brick construction.

There were also two barracks for the officers, 20-by-90 feet in size, of frame construction. A relatively elaborate brick building served as dwelling and headquarters for the commandant.

Three mannequins are shown in characteristic dress engaged in typical activities of the soldier off duty.

18. The Fort Pitt Museum Displays a Historic Cannon

This beautiful cannon is one of four that were given by Marquis de LaFayette to his friend, George Washington, for the use of the Continental Army. LaFayette purchased these cannon in France while recuperating from wounds he suffered in the Battle of Brandywine. They were used continuously in the Revolution and through the Siege of Yorktown. After the war all four cannon were given to the Commonwealth of Pennsylvania. They were recently turned over to the Pennsylvania Historical and Museum Commission by whom this one was given to the Fort Pitt Museum (see illustration, p. 57).

The cannon was cast in bronze in Strasbourg in the 1760's and bears the name "La Trompette." It is mounted on a wooden garrison carriage built from a drawing prepared from 18th century records.

20. Soldiers Had a Personal Pride in Their Powder Horns

The powder horn was frequently used by the 18th century soldier and settler. The hollowed-out cow's horn was uniquely adapted to this use. It was light, strong, water- and flame-proof, and its natural curve fitted the shape of the body. Powder horns were sometimes decorated with designs scratched into the surface, known as *scrimshaw work.* These designs are fascinating as folk art and sometimes histori-cally important. As mementoes of their military campaign these horns were prized by the soldiers and became cherished heirlooms of their descendants.

The Fort Pitt powder horn was owned by Archibald Woodside of North Carolina while at Fort Pitt and dated 1758. The lines, rein-forced with black and brown stains, show the British coat-of-arms, various flags and articles of war, and a hunter pursuing a stag, hare, and boar. Note the Forks of the Ohio with *Fort Pitt* and the *Ohio Riviere.*

The other horn portrays Fort Cumberland, now Cumberland, Maryland, on the Potomac River, the base of Braddock's expedition to the Ohio Country. Note the turkey and other small birds, the crown with GR beneath it and, most surprisingly, two mermaids. The horn bears the inscription: *John Huradon, His Horn, Made at Fort Cumberland.*

21. The Swivel Gun Was Useful to an Army on the Move

The swivel gun because of its comparatively light weight was adapted for use in the field. It could be readily mounted on a tree stump or improvised rampart and moved about as required for emer-gency action in attack or defense. This is an authentic reproduction of an 18th century original. The visitor is invited to rotate or elevate the cannon by hand, as it was manipulated in real action.

22. Mercer's Fort Weathered a Grave Dilemma

Forbes and his army returned east in late November 1758. Six weeks later Colonel Hugh Mercer had finished a fort that could house 400 men. Upon this small garrison was placed the brave responsibility of resisting any French counterattack until mid-1759, by which time troops and supplies could be brought from Philadelphia to build the fort that William Pitt had ordered, to maintain "the undisputed possession of the Ohio."

The ominous rumors of early spring had by mid-July become a certainty. A large French force was being assembled at Fort Machault (present-day Franklin), only two days by river from the Point. Facing certain annihilation, Mercer destroyed the buildings outside the fort. As he was preparing to burn the fort itself and retreat across the Monongahela, he received joyful news. On July 12, just as the 1,500

56

Actual Cannon presented to the Continental Army by Marquis de LaFayette — Exhibit 18

(*page 55*)

French and Indians were about to descend the Allegheny to attack Mercer's frail stronghold, they received a frantic summons to relieve the siege of Fort Niagara. They returned north posthaste only to be decisively routed by the British when but a mile from Fort Niagara. Thus the little garrison of Mercer's Fort was spared the test of war.

Mercer's Fort was small and crowded — ". . . huddled up in a very hasty manner," as Colonel Hugh Mercer described it. Located on the Monongahela shore about 1,000 feet above the ruins of Fort Duquesne, the fort was a square formed by log buildings which were joined at their ends by stockaded bastions measuring 150 feet from tip to tip. This improvised and poor stronghold proclaimed British control of the Forks of the Ohio through eight precarious months.

23A. The British Officer Was Ill-Prepared for the Wilderness Life

The British officer was a gentleman. He was not at home in the American wilderness and was unacquainted with frontier warfare. Although entitled to certain privileges he preserved only a few of the amenities of the officer's life in England. At times he fared little better than the enlisted man.

This exhibit includes the following original artifacts (see illustration, p. 59). A rare, engraved, all-steel flintlock pistol made in Scotland about 1750 by I. O. Shiels. It exemplifies the superb craftsmanship of the Scottish gunsmith. A fine silver-mounted Queen Anne style flintlock pistol, about 1720. A basket-hilted broadsword, made in Scotland about 1650 by Andrea Ferara. While not of the French and Indian War period, such fine and serviceable weapons, often family heirlooms, were proudly carried by Scottish officers. A hunting sword, commonly used by civilians in the mid-18th century. While never used as a military weapon in combat, such swords were frequently worn by army officers as a symbol of rank.

Portable, demountable candlesticks which unscrewed for convenience in carrying. No other illumination was available except from the fireplace. A wooden chest used by officers to store and transport personal articles. They also served as seats in hut or tent. Oversized supports prevented the chest from sinking into earthen floor when wet or muddy. A leather dispatch case for important papers, tooled and stitched by hand. Messengers traveled the forest paths with important military communications in such cases. A handsome engraved salt horn with silver chain attests to the importance attached to a personal salt

58

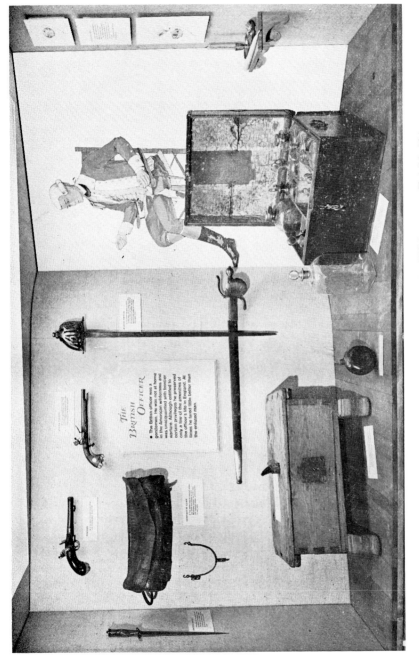

The British Officers carried many Possessions into the Wilderness — Exhibit 23-A

(*page 58*)

ration. Salt was scarce and valuable in the wilderness. A wine chest or portable wine cellar. The bottles in this fitted field case served to cheer the owner in the cold and loneliness of the forest campaign. The exhibit also contains a spur, a pewter canteen and a European sword.

23B. The British Soldier Did Not Welcome His American Service

For the typical British enlisted man, there was no glamor to serving in the hostile, unsettled, and wild country. The army issue of uniform, weapons and gear was not standardized. A soldier had to make do with what he was given and with what he could improvise.

The case contains a collection of genuine personal arms and articles, including a bullet mold, a clasp knife, and bayonet.

The British infantry musket was affectionately called the "Brown Bess" after Queen Elizabeth. Three different models were made. Displayed here is a rare sample of the first model used before 1760. It has a 46" barrel and is .55 calibre. Pole arms, pikes and spontoons were not intended for combat. They were carried as a flag or banner at the head of a company. Here we see American pole arms that were carried by American troops attached to British regulars. A pouch and horn carried by the militia. Lead shot was carried in the leather pouch, powder in the horn. A knife and a powder measure were fitted to the case. An American flintlock. American troops who fought beside British regulars carried a variety of muskets. This long American-made flintlock is typical of those muskets.

23C. The Frontier Scout Was a Unique American Breed

The regular troops were well disciplined and most dependable in the type of European warfare to which they were accustomed. But in wilderness fighting in America they were at a great disadvantage. Bouquet wrote that ". . . I cannot think of employing Regular Troops alone, who are totally unacquainted with the Woods, and unable to Flank or Reconnoitre without the Assistance of Woodsmen to procure Intelligence ; . . ." These woodsmen, or scouts, also served as the "expresses" who carried the vital military dispatches through forests infested with hostile Indians, as, for instance, during the siege of Fort Pitt and the Battle of Bushy Run. They often served without regulation uniform but wore the clothes they brought from home or farm.

23D. 18th Century Ordnance Was Varied and Picturesque

This case contains some rare and precious relics of another time (see illustration, p. 62). Among these are two huge muskets. Having too much weight and recoil to be fired from the shoulder, they were rested upon the rampart wall and hence were called "wall pieces." The upper one is a French piece, which weighs 25 pounds and could also be supported on a single pole rest by means of the swivel and pivot attachment. It is of .75 calibre, has a rifled barrel and is dated 1744.

Below it is a British wall piece used in the latter half of the 18th century. It is of .94 calibre and weighs 22 pounds. The metal projection on the bottom of the barrel was hooked over the edge of the wall on which the musket rested and served to break the recoil.

On the case bottom stands a beautiful 18th century bronze cannon which came from Clumber Hall in England. It is finely cast and wrought with bands of foliage and the arms, crest and initial of Henry Fiennes Clinton, second Duke of Newcastle. The wooden carriage is original though slightly restored. Note the applied rosettes and scrolls and the iron wheels with lion's mask hubs. This cannon was bought at auction in London in 1968.

24A. Fort Pitt Had Its Severest Test in the Siege of Pontiac's War

When France ceded her American possessions in February of 1763, the Indians had been led to expect that all British soldiers would be withdrawn from the frontier. Instead, the French forts were occupied or replaced by the British, and Fort Pitt was obviously not temporary. An even greater menace to the Indians was the never-ending occupation of their hunting grounds by the settlers. These, and other grievances, led to the Indian uprising of 1763 named for the principal leader, Pontiac's War.

By secret arrangement among the Indian tribes all posts west of Lake Erie were attacked simultaneously in May. The only places that held out over the next three months were Detroit, Fort Pitt, Fort Ligonier, Fort Bedford, Carlisle and Fort Augusta. The map at the bottom of the case shows the area included in Pontiac's War. Nearly 100 traders were murdered and their goods confiscated. All homes and settlements outside the forts were destroyed, rendering over 1,000 families homeless.

In addition to the garrison of 300, the barracks of Fort Pitt were

Unusual and genuine Artifacts of 18th-century Armament — Exhibit 23D

(*page 61*)

crammed with 100 men, women and children brought in from the village of Pittsburgh. The Indians, concealed in the riverbank, maintained a continuous sniper fire. Flames resulting from their fire arrows were quenched by bucket brigades and an improvised fire engine.

The siege, extending from May 27 to August 9, was climaxed in the last four days of July by a "most furious fire from all Quarters on the Fort," in spite of which only one person was killed. Seven were wounded, including the commandant, Captain Simeon Ecuyer.

The appearance of Fort Pitt while under siege is shown in a water-color painting looking toward the Allegheny River from the Ohio Bastion. This view is based upon early fort plans, military correspondence and accounts (see illustration, p. 65).

The Ohio Bastion, which stood nearest the Allegheny River, was partially carried away by the spring floods. It was never entirely rebuilt, hence it was known as the "Low Bastion." To protect this vulnerable face of the fort, an improvised rampart was formed of wooden stockades, patched with bales of furs, barrels, and other objects. The buildings of the Lower Town, between the fort and the river, were destroyed to deprive the enemy of cover.

Three other paintings re-create three important incidents of the siege. The first incident near the fort was the murder on May 29 of two soldiers at the Saw Mill which gave its name to present-day Saw Mill Run Boulevard. The previous day William Clapham and his family had been massacred at their cabin on the Youghiogheny River.

On June 22 a party of Indians appeared in the limits of the cleared area before the fort, drove off the horses and killed most of the cattle. The Indians were dispersed by howitzer fire from the fort.

The only major battle of the siege occurred not in the fort but on a forested hill near the little stream, Bushy Run, some 30 miles west of Fort Pitt where the Indians sought to intercept and destroy the army approaching to lift the siege.

The arrival of Colonel Henry Bouquet on August 10 was a joyful occasion for the beleaguered garrison and for Bouquet's troops who had lost eight officers and 115 men in the decisive defeat of the Indians at Bushy Run. In this picture Captain Simeon Ecuyer, commandant of Fort Pitt, greets the indomitable Bouquet.

24B. Bushy Run Was the Decisive Battle of Pontiac's War

Colonel Henry Bouquet was provided with 500 soldiers and a wagon train of supplies and ordered to lift the siege of Fort Pitt. He arrived at Fort Ligonier on August 2, 1763, where he left most of his wagons and baggage and hastened forward with pack horses and supplies for the beleaguered garrison. He encountered the Indians in a two-day battle on August 5 and 6 which proved to be the turning point of Pontiac's War. But for this the people at Fort Pitt would have had shortly to submit to massacre by the Indians.

Bouquet's letters to Lord Jeffery Amherst of August 5 and 6 provide the most reliable and stirring account of the engagement. When the advance guard was attacked about one o'clock, the English repeatedly drove off the Indians but "as soon as they were driven from one Post they appeared on another till by continual Reinforcements they were at last able to surround us . . ." The advance guard marched back to protect the baggage train. The intense fighting lasted until nightfall with a loss of sixty killed or wounded. Bouquet praised the "cool and Steady behavior of the Troops . . ." That night the troops were collected on high ground and the wounded placed behind breastworks formed with bags of flour.

"In the morning the Savages surrounded our Camp . . . Shouting and yelping . . ." Though the Indians made repeated unsuccessful efforts to penetrate the camp, they "always gave way when pressed and appeared again Immediately." The troops were exhausted from marching and battle fatigue and were "Distressed to the last Degree by a Total Want of Water much more Intolerable than the Enemy's Fire . . ."

Bouquet realized his only hope of success was in luring the Indians into the open. By a masterly stratagem he rearranged his troops so that ". . . the Barbarians mistaking these motions for a Retreat hurried headlong on, . . ." into the space vacated by the troops. The British then attacked the Indians head-on just as two companies that had been concealed behind the hill drove into the flank of the Indian forces, creating confusion and panic among them. The Indians shortly after fled the field. Bouquet justifiably boasted that ". . . the most Warlike of the savage Tribes have lost their Boasted Claim of being Invincible in the Woods."

The case contains two dioramas. The first shows the "Flour Bag Fort" in which Bouquet's desperate forces sought refuge on the first night of the battle. The second shows the next day's action and the feint of simulated retreat by which Bouquet induced the Indians to charge into the open where they were flanked and utterly routed.

Improvised Ramparts of Ohio Bastion during Siege of Pontiac's War — Exhibit 24A

(*page 63*)

65

The army engineer, Thomas Hutchins, made careful topographic drawings of the battle site. A reproduction of this drawing is displayed here. A detailed section of the map, with an overlay showing the movement of troops during the second day's engagement, is shown on the bottom of the case.

Visitors may today visit the site of this battle which has been set aside as a historic area by the Commonwealth.

24C. Colonel Bouquet Was Unequaled as an Indian Fighter

After the siege of Fort Pitt was ended in August of 1763 the Indians retreated westward. But by early 1764 they renewed their raids on the western frontiers of Virginia and Pennsylvania. Whereupon the hero of the Battle of Bushy Run, Colonel Henry Bouquet, was called upon once more to quell the Indians. This remarkable man again demonstrated his mastery of wilderness warfare. In October of 1764 he led an army of 1,500 deep into the Indian country of what is now Ohio.

Completely cowed, the Indians did not dare to attack these men who knew how to fight in the woods. When the leading chiefs came to Bouquet with offers of submission, he demanded the return of all captives within twelve days.

A beautiful diorama set in a beech forest (see illustration, p. 67) shows Bouquet at his camp near the forks of the Muskingum River, where more than 100 white captives were delivered by the Indians. There were many dramatic and often pathetic scenes as many of the captives had become deeply attached to their Indian "relations," whose way of life they had accepted. Bouquet's Ohio expedition ended the Indian wars in Pennsylvania and the upper Ohio.

24D. Wayne Ended Forever Indian Wars in This Area

In 1792 General Anthony Wayne was commissioned to organize and train an army to end the Indian menace, once and for all. Secretary of War General Knox was instructed by President George Washington to build in Pittsburgh a base of operations to be known as Fort LaFayette (later shortened to Fayette), in honor of his French friend of Revolutionary days. Fort Fayette was the fifth and last fort to be built within the triangle of downtown Pittsburgh. It lay across Penn Avenue at 10th Street, and is shown by an aerial view based on early military drawings and records (see illustration, p. 69).

Colonel Henry Bouquet presides over the Return of Indian Captives — Exhibit 24C

(*page 66*)

As the morale of his men suffered from the distractions of the city, Wayne relocated his camp at Legionville, near modern Ambridge. Here he applied the intensive training and discipline which resulted in the decisive defeat of the Indians near Sandusky in 1794 at the battle of Fallen Timbers, shown in the painting.

A garrison was retained at Fort Fayette until the War of 1812, when it rendered assistance to Commodore Perry as a base for supplies, purchase of horses and training of soldiers. Many British prisoners were sent to the fort after Perry's victory. The property was sold and garrison removed in 1815.

A most effective weapon in the war upon the Indians was the field howitzer. An authentic replica of a 2¾" U.S. howitzer is shown in this case. It could be carried with its carriage by a pack horse. Wayne called them his "flying Howitzers" . . . "the only kind of Artillery that can be transported with ease & used with effect against savages . . ." in wooded mountainous country without roads.

25. The Gateway to the West Becomes the Workshop of the World

The illustrations in this case provide glimpses of various facets of early Pittsburgh. As a city, Pittsburgh was slow to mature because it remained a garrison town until after the War of 1812. But Pittsburgh's location at the head of navigation to the vast inland basin made it a funnel through which poured one of the greatest migrations of people in history. In this movement the Ohio River carried 18,000 pioneers in the single year 1788. By 1830 one-third of the American people, some 3½ million, lived west of the mountains.

As methods and routes of transportation were developed, industry and commerce in the Pittsburgh region were continually accelerated. Iron furnaces, forges, and mills sent manufactured goods north, west, south, and, with the coming of canals and railroads, east. By the mid-19th century, with the discovery of the undreamed-of potentialities of its natural resources in oil and gas and with the fuller utilization of its coal deposits, the Pittsburgh region stood on the threshold of the still greater industrial era that made it famous as the Workshop of the World.

26. Distinguished Houses Soon Appeared in Western Pennsylvania

Few houses of substantial or distinguished character were built in this district before the 1780's, by which time relative peace had been

Fort Fayette once lay across present-day Penn Avenue at 10th Street — Exhibit 24D

Conjectural Restoration Drawing by Charles M. Stotz

(page 66)

established and commerce and industry had begun to flourish. The first settlers came mostly from Maryland and Virginia. They built homes in the rural areas of what is now southwestern Pennsylvania. The architectural character of their houses almost invariably reflect the character of the buildings they had known in their places of origin.

In the design of this room (see illustration, p. 71) the architect has utilized details from four existing dwellings, built between 1785 and 1815, in Washington, Westmoreland, Fayette, and Allegheny Counties. The room is furnished with period pieces that a well-to-do owner of the time might import from the eastern cities.

27. The Period from 1850 to 1950 Was the Age of Industry

By 1850 the foundations of Pittsburgh's future industrial greatness had been laid. Coke replaced charcoal as fuel for the furnaces. Railroads brought rich iron ore from the west. River coal outcrops were tapped. Industry moved to the river valleys and into the city itself. River traffic steadily increased. Pioneer flatboats and keelboats were replaced with great fleets of barges pushed by stern wheel steamboats. Steel mills, foundries, glass plants and factories of all kinds filled "The Workshop of the World" with smoke, noise and bustling activity.

The ever-increasing demand for labor was met by hordes of immigrant workers from Europe. Industrial growth was accompanied by economic ills and social inequalities. Unrest in labor circles climaxed in the Railroad Strike of 1877 and the Homestead Steel Strike of 1892. In spite of these protests, concern with production and profits was not tempered with a recognition of the need for economic and social reforms until well into the 20th century. This case contains reproductions of early drawings and a painting of a characteristic Pittsburgh hillside with dwellings of the working classes clinging to the steep slopes and a Victorian mansion of the well-to-do on the summit.

By the middle of this century, however, Pittsburgh attracted worldwide attention with its "renaissance" and became a model for other cities to follow in planning for a better environment for living and working. Pittsburgh had progressed through three periods of pioneering effort. First, in the establishment of the Gateway to the West in the 18th century. Then in the development of commerce and industry in the 19th century. And finally in the striving for urban development in the 20th century.

Fine Houses were built in the late 1700's in southwestern Pennsylvania — Exhibit 26

(*page 68*)

71

	1850	*1900*
Population of Pittsburgh	79,873	321,616
Population of Allegheny County	138,290	775,058
Area of Pittsburgh	1,130 acres	17,952 acres
	1,766 sq. mi.	28,051 sq. mi.
Pittsburgh's annual glass production	$1.0 million	$2.5 million
Pittsburgh's annual steel production	$6.5 million	$90.8 million

28A. The Streams Were Dotted with Grist Mills

Flour was first ground in querns, small mills powered by hand or horse. Almost every creek in the district with adequate fall and water volume was provided with a grist mill. The mill erected for George Washington at Perryopolis in 1744-45 was almost certainly the first water-power mill with burr millstones west of the mountains. By 1810 western Pennsylvania contained nearly 600 mills.

This case contains photographs of early grist mills taken from *The Early Architecture of Western Pennsylvania* (see illustration, p. 73). Also a model of grist mill machinery which explains the method of operation. A genuine early burr stone is accompanied by a drawing showing the process of dressing the stone with the following explanation:

The miller had to shut down occasionally to re-cut the dulled grooves in the working surfaces of his millstones with a very hard chisel-headed hammer called a millbill. Itinerant stone dressers also did the work, taking six to eight days to resharpen a pair of stones. The grooves had what might be called a check-mark profile, one side nearly vertical, the other sloping. They were arranged variously but always in such a way that the upper ones would shear across the lower, with the steeper edges opposed to achieve a cutting action. The commonest arrangement was in groups of straight grooves, each group parallel to a tangent of the central hole. The runner, or rotating upper stone, was just slightly concave. The bedder, or lower fixed stone, was convex but was almost imperceptibly flatter than the runner. This made the stone beds closest at their outer edges and therefore grind finest there.

28B. Printing Flourished in Early Pittsburgh

The *Pittsburgh Gazette,* launched in 1786 by John Scull, was the first newspaper west of the mountains. Type and press (similar to the

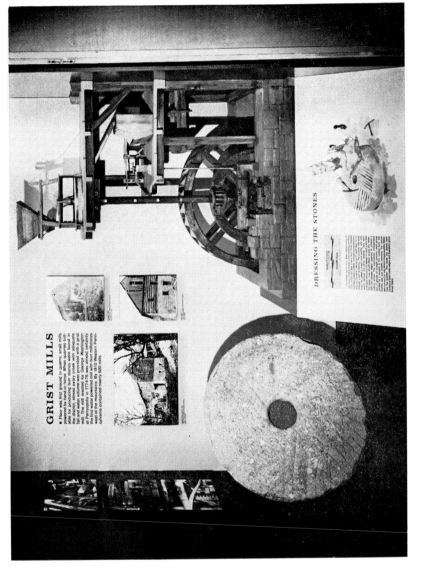

Scale Model of an early Grist Mill with its burr stone — Exhibit 28A

(page 72)

completely accurate quarter-scale model shown in the case) were brought from Philadelphia. By 1800 there were six other papers, all weeklies, consisting of a sheet of four pages and smaller than the modern "tabloid."

The cost and scarcity of paper was relieved by the building in 1797 of a water-powered paper mill at Brownsville. The first volume of Hugh Henry Brackenridge's *Modern Chivalry* (and the first book printed in Pittsburgh) was published here in 1793. By 1815, Zadok Cramer had published some seventy books and pamphlets, including the *Pittsburgh Almanack* and *The Navigator*.

The case contains a series of drawings showing the successive steps in operating a press. Also included are an ink "dauber," a frame of the type locked in place and several examples of early printing, including one of the first issues of the *Pittsburgh Gazette*.

28C. Ocean-going Ships Were Built Here Between 1792 and 1810

Before the great turnpike building days of the 1830's conveyance of produce over the poor mountain roads to the eastern markets was costly and slow. Transportation by water was faster and cheaper. Because of Pittsburgh's position at the head of navigation on the Ohio River, boat building was an important industry from the first. Thousands of rafts, flatboats, keelboats and other craft carried pioneers and produce to the great inland markets. In fact, between 1792 and 1810 over twenty ocean-going ships were built in the Pittsburgh region to take surplus produce via the Ohio and Mississippi Rivers to the east coast and to foreign markets as well.

One such ship was the schooner, the *Monongahela Farmer,* shown in this diorama in the process of construction (see illustration, p. 75). It was built in 1801 at Elizabeth on the Monongahela River as the cooperative venture of a group of local farmers. Keelboats and flatboats may be seen in the background.

28D. The Glass Industry Had an Early Start in This District

Glass was a rare and precious commodity in the early days on the frontier because of the cost of transporting it over the mountains. The first glass plant west of the mountains was established by O'Hara and Craig in 1797 in Pittsburgh at the foot of Mount Washington. Coal from the outcrops on the hill above was used as fuel. Another glass plant was built the same year by Albert Gallatin near Brownsville.

74

Ocean-going Ships were built at Elizabeth on the Monongahela River — Exhibit 28C

(page 74)

75

Sand, lead and clay for melting-pots had to be imported from the east and even from Europe. The first successful flint glass works in America was developed in Pittsburgh by Benjamin Bakewell in 1808. Bakewell glass was of such high quality that it was shipped by river and sea to supply the lucrative markets in eastern America and Europe. By 1815 there were five glass works in Pittsburgh.

This exhibit shows early glass-blowing methods, tools of the craft and samples of glassware.

28E.   *The Early Charcoal Iron Industry Was a Rural Activity*

The first iron furnace in western Pennsylvania was built in 1790. By 1800 there were eleven furnaces in the region, most of them near Chestnut Ridge, where the following necessary conditions were best met.

1: Natural iron ore deposits. 2: Limestone to use for flux. 3: Water power to operate the blast. 4: Roads or navigable streams to market the products. 5: Vast stands of timber for making charcoal. (An acre of timber yielding enough charcoal for only one day's operation.)

Furnaces produced such items as cast iron kettles, stove plates, firebacks, and cannon balls but, of greatest importance, the bulk or "pig" iron which was sent to forges where iron was shaped into many products.

The exhibit includes a cut-away view of a charcoal iron furnace that explains the various elements of water power, blast bellows, charging of the furnace and the casting beds. Also included are photographs of early iron furnaces of the district and samples of finished articles of iron.

IV. THE MODEL OF FORT PITT

THE 16-FOOT-WIDE well in the center of the William Pitt Memorial Hall contains a model of Fort Pitt, made to the scale of ten feet to the inch. See the illustration on pages 88 and 89. The plan of Fort Pitt on page 79 identifies the principal features of the fort which are mentioned in the following pages. The area covered by the model includes all of the land within the Point up to Commonwealth Place and the Hilton Hotel. Earphones are provided so that the visitor viewing the model may listen to a taped narration describing the fort. He will thus be better prepared to understand the museum exhibits, many of which explain the design and construction of the fort, its main features and the events that transpired there. The research and planning involved in making the model is described on page 86. The construction of this model was made possible by a grant from the Buhl Foundation of Pittsburgh.

How Fort Pitt Came to Be Built at the Point

The site of Point State Park was first occupied by Fort Duquesne and its little village. From 1754 to 1758 only French was spoken at the Forks of the Ohio. When the British seized the Point in November of 1758 they proclaimed undisputed control of the headwaters of the Ohio by building Fort Pitt, their most elaborate fortress on the American frontier. Fort Pitt was large enough to contain seventeen forts the size of Fort Duquesne! The British found Fort Duquesne in ruins as the French had destroyed their fort by fire and explosives before they left. Colonel Hugh Mercer was ordered immediately to build a small temporary fort to hold the Forks of the Ohio while Captain Harry Gordon went to Philadelphia to assemble materials and recruit workmen for the construction of Fort Pitt. Captain Gordon is generally credited with the design of Fort Pitt and it was he who directed its construction, by order of General Stanwix, from 1759 to 1761.

The site to be selected for Fort Pitt was the subject of much controversy. The Point area was condemned by many because of the flood hazard. In fact, serious consideration was given McKee's Rocks Hill as the fort site, as described in Exhibit 8A shown on page 25. But when General John Stanwix arrived in Pittsburgh he finally determined that the strategic command of the three rivers outweighed any and all objections to the Point site, including the hazard of inundation. However, after the disastrous floods of 1762 and 1763, Lt. Col. Wm. Eyre was sent by General Amherst to assess the damage to Fort Pitt and recommend the possible relocation of the fort, even at this late date. Although Eyre again spoke in favor of the McKee's Rocks Hill or possibly the heights on which Duquesne University now stands, it was found more expedient to repair and retain Fort Pitt, which had been substantially completed.

Fort Pitt with Its Outworks Was a Complex Structure

The pentagonal form of Fort Pitt was admirably adapted to the triangular shape of the site. The fort proper lay very close to the Monongahela bank so as to occupy the higher ground on that side and also to provide space on the lower ground of some 4.8 acres between the fort and the Allegheny River. This protected building area, known as the Low Town (see plan on page 79), contained a helter-skelter collection of cabins, shacks and storage buildings, occupied by artisans, traders, workmen, contractors, and other civilians. The military found it difficult to establish discipline among these unruly people. The village was razed during Pontiac's War to deprive the Indians of cover.

A continuous ditch, known as "The Isthmus," extended in front of the land side of the fort from the Allegheny almost to the Monongahela River. The five-sided fort was surrounded by a ditch or moat which was filled with water only at high stages of the river. This ditch joined the Isthmus at two points. The Isthmus was paralleled by the earth embankments, known as the Epaulement, which provided protection for an advance line of soldiers. The entrance road to the fort crossed the ditch at two points by bridges, each protected at their inner end by drawbridges that were lifted at night. The triangular island or ravelin between these bridges served as added protection for the entrance and contained an underground guardroom for prisoners. There was another ravelin of simpler type between the Grenadier and Flag Bastions and still another which commanded the Monongahela River opposite the Monongahela Curtain.

Bastions projected from each of the five corners of the fort proper. The five bastions, as well as the five curtain walls which connected the bastions, are designated by names given on the fort plan, page 79.

78

PLAN OF FORT PITT, WITH NAMES OF ITS VARIOUS PAR
Note comparative sizes of Fort Duquesne and Mercer's F

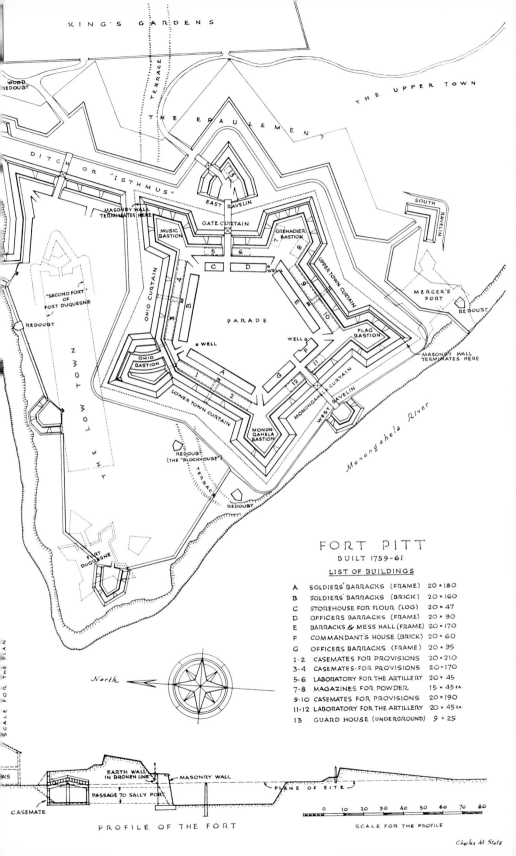

KING'S GARDENS

WOOD
REDOUBT

TERRACE

THE UPPER TOWN

THE ERAULEMENT

DITCH OR "ISTHMUS"

MASONRY WALL
TERMINATES HERE

EAST RAVELIN

SOUTH
RAVELIN

MUSIC
BASTION

GATE CURTAIN

GRENADIER
BASTION

MERCER'S
FORT

REDOUBT

"SECOND FORT"
OF
FORT DUQUESNE

OHIO CURTAIN

UPPER TOWN CURTAIN

PARADE

WELL

REDOUBT

OHIO
BASTION

WELL

FLAG
BASTION

MASONRY WALL
TERMINATES HERE

THE LOW TOWN

WELL

LOWER TOWN CURTAIN

MONONGAHELA CURTAIN

WEST RAVELIN

MONON-
GAHELA
BASTION

Monongahela River

REDOUBT
(THE "BLOCKHOUSE")

TERRACE

REDOUBT

FORT
DUQUESNE

FORT PITT
BUILT 1759-61
LIST OF BUILDINGS

A	SOLDIERS' BARRACKS (FRAME)	20 × 180
B	SOLDIERS' BARRACKS (BRICK)	20 × 160
C	STOREHOUSE FOR FLOUR (LOG)	20 × 47
D	OFFICERS BARRACKS (FRAME)	20 × 90
E	BARRACKS & MESS HALL (FRAME)	20 × 170
F	COMMANDANT'S HOUSE (BRICK)	20 × 60
G	OFFICERS BARRACKS (FRAME)	20 × 95
1-2	CASEMATES FOR PROVISIONS	20 × 210
3-4	CASEMATES FOR PROVISIONS	20 × 170
5-6	LABORATORY FOR THE ARTILLERY	20 × 45
7-8	MAGAZINES FOR POWDER	15 × 45 EA.
9-10	CASEMATES FOR PROVISIONS	20 × 190
11-12	LABORATORY FOR THE ARTILLERY	20 × 45 EA.
13	GUARD HOUSE (UNDERGROUND)	9 × 25

North

SCALE FOR THE PLAN

EARTH WALL
IN BROKEN LINE

MASONRY WALL

PLANE OF SITE

PASSAGE TO SALLY PORT

CASEMATE

PROFILE OF THE FORT

0 10 20 30 40 50 60 70 80

SCALE FOR THE PROFILE

Charles M. Stotz

The distance from tip to tip of the bastions varied from 416 to 476 feet. The total area within the ramparts contained 2.1 acres and the parade ground within the fort about 1.3 acres. The entire fort, with its outworks, not including the gardens, occupied 17.6 acres. Sentries walked nearly a half mile in making a complete circuit of the ramparts.

The Masonry Walls of Fort Pitt Were Extensive and Costly

Fort Pitt was a "dirt fort." In simplest terms it was a five-sided parade ground, bordered by five rows of buildings, which, in turn, were protected by five parallel mounds of earth shaped to the contours of the conventional rampart of the day.

On the two sides toward the land or eastern face, these earth ramparts were supported by heavy walls faced with brick and backed up with stone, resting upon stone footings and surmounted by a cap piece of stone. This fifteen-foot-high brick facing, or revetment, enclosed the Music Bastion and extended southward around the Flag Bastion. The tips of these brick walls were trimmed with hewn stone. The nature of these walls may be seen in the actual remains of the Music Bastion where a path around permits the visitor to examine the wall at close quarters. This stout wall was never called upon to resist the artillery fire for which it was designed, but it saved the fort from destruction by resisting the flood currents of 1762 and 1763 when the water rose seven feet above the parade ground. The earthen bastions and shore line ramparts suffered great damage in these floods and were never entirely repaired.

The Monongahela Bastion, which contains the Fort Pitt Museum, was originally an earth structure but was constructed of brick ramparts for obviously practical reasons, and conforms with the character of the brick bastions on the eastern or land side of the fort. Those in command later regretted that the entire fort was not faced with brick to withstand better the flood waters.

The Ramparts of the Fort Contained Many Underground Rooms

A careful measurement of the plans shows that some 66,000 cubic yards of earth, excavated to form the ditches, was used in the construction of the fort walls, a formidable building operation for those days of hand labor when our modern earth-moving machinery was unknown. A considerable saving in the earth needed for the structure was effected by the construction of casemates and magazines within the curtains and the bastions. These underground structures were sunk from five to seven feet below the level of the parade ground. These casemates and the use to which they were put as powder magazines, artillery laboratories (see Exhibit 15A, page 51), and provisions are indicated on the fort plan, page 79. In all there were about 745 feet of casemates, averaging twenty feet in width.

Earthworks of the fort were subject to serious deterioration not only from frosts, thaws and rains but from grazing horses and cattle as well as smaller animals. The records contain many references to this subject. Chickens and hogs were forbidden in the ditches and banks of the fort, and, in the late days, the inhabitants were even prohibited from digging for worms. Bouquet ordered that after February 15, 1764, "all dogs & fowls seen upon the Rampart to be Killed."

The Parade Ground Was Bordered by Seven Buildings

The three barracks within the fort were two stories high. The barracks behind the Lower Town Curtain, the only one built of brick, was 190 by 20 feet in size. This was used for many years after the two wood barracks had become untenable. These barracks housed between 700 and 1,000 men in relative comfort, for frontier days, as seen in Exhibit 17 on page 54. As one entered the parade through the main entrance, the squared log building for bulk storage of flour stood on the right and the frame officers' barracks on the left. Behind the Monongahela Curtain stood a frame officers' barracks on the right and the Commandant's house on the left. This latter building was of brick and excited the admiration of the Quaker storekeeper, Kenny, who mentioned its "fine Steps at yᵉ Door of Hewn free Stone, a Cellar all under it . . ."

The fort was not officially named by General Stanwix until November of 1759. Work was begun on September 3. It was not until the summer of 1760 that men were allowed to rest on Sundays. Because of the difficulty in obtaining currency the men were given daily rations of liquor. Until the rum and whisky were available there had been illness "owing to drinking quantities of bad Water." Lay workers, or "artificers," were employed in many of the specialized crafts, there being at least 128 of them still at work after October 1760.

The Fort Was Surrounded by Extensive Work Areas

The area outside the fort was a beehive of activity. The preparation and assembling of materials and the building of boats spread operations a great distance from the building site and necessitated covering parties to protect the men at work. Desirable timber within easy reach was soon depleted. Forage brought in for the horses had to be supplemented with hay and grain locally grown some distance up the rivers. Coal miners were at work on the slopes of Mount Washington and stone quarries on the slopes of the hill now occupied by Duquesne University. Clay and shales were excavated for use in the brick kilns, fired with charcoal or coal. Limestone was reduced in kilns for the making of plaster and mortar. These activities occupied much of the ground near the fort not occupied by piles of building materials, saw pits, ovens, forges, blacksmith and cooper shops and the crude buildings to house the workers and horses. A saw mill across the river gave Saw Mill Run its name. The efficient and harmonious direction of this motley organization was a constant challenge to both the engineers and the officers who directed them.

Many officers and members of the artillery lived outside the fort in settlements that extended along the Monongahela shore.

The river banks were crowded with river craft and depots for receiving supplies and materials sent down the Monongahela from Redstone, present-day Brownsville, where goods, foodstuffs and animals were delivered from the south.

The Severest Test of Fort Pitt Was in Pontiac's Siege

Captain Simeon Ecuyer was hard pressed during the siege of Fort Pitt in 1763 to make his badly damaged parapets proof even against the poor fire and arrows of the Indians. By this time pickets had replaced the missing parapets on the earth ramparts and an improvised parapet of planks was used on the brick front. In some places Ecuyer was reduced to the expedient of placing his men behind bales of furs and skins taken from the trading store. For further protection stockades were placed at the base of the earth scarp walls (see illustration on page 65).

During the two-month siege of Pontiac's War the people and most of the animals were brought within the fort. All outlying buildings, including the Low Town, were razed. Though the Indians did not attack in military fashion, they maintained a continuous and deadly sniper fire from the cover of the river banks. Temporary barricades were hastily erected on the earth ramparts that had been injured by

View of the Fort Pitt Model from the Allegheny River shore

83

the floods. For these reasons Colonel Henry Bouquet, after the war, ordered the erection of five redoubts, four of brick and one of timber, to cover the banks and outlying areas. These redoubts stood outside the ramparts of Fort Pitt. One of these redoubts remains today, the Blockhouse (see illustration on page 45), the only surviving remnant of the once mighty Fort Pitt.

The Records Tell Little of the Last Days of the Fort

Captain Gordon ordered discontinuance of further work on the fort in April of 1765. By June of 1766 Gordon's report indicated that further repairs were inexpedient and that ". . . something new should be done." The condition of the fort went from bad to worse and the final disposition of the land and materials dragged on for years. It is difficult to determine just when all vestiges of the fort finally disappeared. The early comments on the subject are scattered and unintelligible for most part. But certainly by 1800 Fort Pitt was indeed a thing of the past.

No records provide a reliable evidence on the cost of Fort Pitt. The writer searched in vain among the archives in London for information on the subject, but he prepared a reasonably careful cost analysis of the fort structure as shown in contemporary drawings and references. It is estimated that to reproduce the fort and its outworks by building methods of 1970 would cost not less than three million dollars. If the hand-labor methods of 1761 were employed, the cost would be much higher.

Why Was Fort Pitt So Elaborate?

Another question frequently asked is, "Why did the British government order the construction of a fort of such great size and elaboration?" Judging by informed hindsight, Fort Pitt was not unreasonably large, considering the fact that a return of the French in numbers and with adequate artillery was anticipated during the early days of its construction. And one must recognize that the positive and permanent control of the upper Ohio Valley appeared a desperately important objective to William Pitt when he ordered the building of a fort "in every way adequate to the great importance of the sever¹ objects." England had been waging a losing war for five years; bold strokes were necessary. Had this shrewd leader foreseen the swift and favorable changes of fortune that lay ahead for England he might have been more conservative in his instructions. But if Pitt ever regretted this fine gesture of defense, it was probably seventeen years later when those for whom the fort was built declared their independence from England.

For a fuller account of Fort Pitt and the four other forts which once stood within Pittsburgh's Triangle, the reader is referred to the work "Defense in the Wilderness" which forms a part of *Drums in the Forest*, published in 1958 by The Historical Society of Western Pennsylvania. The writer, who was also author of the above work, has quoted freely from it in this article.

The King's Gardens Formed a Prominent Feature of the Point

Because of limitations in space, the model shows only the western fringe of the King's Gardens which contained about ten acres of cultivated land and extended along the Allegheny River shore between present-day Hilton Hotel and Horne's store. As shown in Meyer's drawing, page 46, the gardens were divided into some seventy-seven separate plots. The great floods of 1762 and 1763 wrought great damage, necessitating a great deal of replacement of fences, crops, trees and other features of the garden. Other drawings of the fort area indicate a variation from the layout in Meyer's plan, but his was evidently the most reliable indication of the intentions of the designers. The original of this drawing is in the Public Record Office in London, a beautiful piece of drafting in ink and color. This ambitious garden scheme was never fully realized because of the floods and gradual relaxation in the work of construction.

The glamorous name, King's Gardens, belies the grim struggle waged by the garrison of Fort Pitt against forest, flood, Indian vandalism, weather and insect pests to provide crops for the survival of man and beast.

Work proceeded intensively on the gardens with the start of fort construction. It is pleasant to note that a deer park was established and that a "new Fence" was being built "across the Big Garden which is to be done very Elegantly," the first hint of refinement on the frontier. It was noted that hogs "continue to break thro' the Fences, And are Continually in the Kings Garden and Fields adjoining." Finally, hogs were prohibited within three miles of the fort lest they be "killed and confiscated for use of the King's Troops." After the flood of 1763, in which "The poor deer's leg was broken," Commandant Ecuyer ordered trees planted and the garden again enclosed against the animals. During Pontiac's War the gardens were easy prey to the besieging Indians. Oxen and cows, placed during the emergency in the deer park, were shot by the Indians and the crops pillaged. In January of 1764 the gardens and fields were again fenced and "ploughed, and sowed with Garden seeds, Corn, Oats, & Speltz." Ecuyer in April mentions new refinements: "the deer park, the little garden, and the bowling green, I am just now making into one garden, it will be extremely pretty and very useful to this garrison, the King's garden will be put in proper order." Later, "we eat sallud from it already several times and Sparrow grass every day from the King's Garden." Bouquet mentioned that "the Men will recover from the Scurvy by the use of such Greens as the gardens can afford them." Efforts to induce the residents, especially those in the Low Town, to raise small gardens of their own met with little success.

A new enemy appeared in the form of a pestilence of locusts and grasshoppers, which "in the King's Garden they destroyed 5,000 cabbage plants, and a great many Seeds of different kinds." During this disaster 10,000 cabbages were planted and another 10,000 ordered while ". . . we have parties constantly in it from 8 in the Morning till 7 in the afternoon to keep off the grasshoppers, nevertheless they do a world of mischief to the plants." However, in September Bouquet reported a sufficient supply of vegetables to supply the garrison through the coming winter.

References to the garden after this time are very few. Brackenridge in 1786 describes an orchard of apple trees and some pear trees among them on the banks of the Allegheny which remained from the old gardens. Zadok Cramer in 1808 mentioned that some of the trees were still bearing fruit.

A somewhat fuller account of the King's Gardens, from which a large part of this material is taken, may be seen in *The Carnegie Magazine* for January 1961, by the same author.

The Model Is Based Upon Early Plans, Records and Conjecture

Fort Pitt was built between the years 1759 and 1761. Almost all vestiges of the fort had disappeared long before 1800. Our only knowledge of Fort Pitt, the most substantial fortification built by the British in America, may be gained only from contemporary plans made by army engineers. These drawings are preserved in English archives, chiefly the Royal Library of Windsor Castle, and in the map rooms of the British Museum and the Public Record office in London. These drawings show the ground layout of the fort and a section through the ramparts of the fort, but provide no drawings to show us what the fort and its buildings looked like. The most complete and reliable of these plans, prepared by army engineer Lt. Elias Meyer in 1761, is reproduced on page 46. After some twenty years of research, including several visits to England, the writer prepared a composite drawing (see page 79) of all information gleaned from the early drawings. From this drawing an enlarged plan at ten feet to the inch was prepared for use in the construction of the model.

To increase its appeal and to provide a proper understanding of original conditions, the model was animated with human figures, animals, outlying buildings, fields, gardens, river craft and landing sites. While some of these features could be determined by a study of the early plans, military correspondence and handbooks, travelers' descriptions, building practice of the time and other records, there were many gaps which had to be filled in by conjecture.

The determination of the original terrain of the Point area was a difficult problem. The topography of the Point was a slightly undulating plane with a terrace about ten feet high parallel with the Allegheny River and about 400 feet from it. This terrace is indicated on the fort plan, page 79. Fort Duquesne was built on the lower shelf thus created, next the Allegheny River. The area of the triangle was then much less, as the shore lines have been pushed out into the rivers in modern times. The present tip of the Point lies today about 430 feet farther down stream than the original one of 1758. The Allegheny River bank now lies about 250 feet and the Monongahela bank about 150 feet beyond their original locations. The old river banks were about twenty feet high and rutted by erosion and irregular in contour.

This Model of Fort Pitt and Environs, Exhibited

William Pitt Memorial Hall, is based on early Maps

Aerial View of Point State Park toward the City

V. POINT STATE PARK, ITS INCEPTION
AND DEVELOPMENT

WITH THE formal opening of the Fort Pitt Museum on June 30, 1969, another significant step had been taken toward the completion of Point State Park. Contracts have been let for razing the Point and Manchester Bridges. Work will then start on the very last phase, the construction of the great basin and fountain at the tip of the Point. The entire area of the downtown Triangle will then focus upon this exciting column of water, rising 150 feet in the air. The removal of the bridges, at long last, will reveal the full and dramatic sweep of the hills and rivers, little changed in their conformation since the white man established himself at the Forks of the Ohio over two hundred years ago. Point State Park will then take its place among the great city parks of the world, unique in its spectacular setting and rich in historical background.

The earliest known proposal for a park at the Point was contained in a book, *A Pleasant Peregrination Through the Prettiest Parts of Pennsylvania,* published in 1836 by Philip H. Nicklin.

"The Pittsburghers have committed an error in not rescuing from the service of Mammon, a triangle of thirty or forty acres at the junction of the Allegheny and Monongahela, and devoting it to the purposes of recreation. It is an unparalleled position for a park in which to ride or walk or sit. Bounded on the right by the clear and rapid Allegheny rushing from New York, and on the left by the deep and slow Monongahela flowing majestically from Virginia, having in front the beginning of the great Ohio, bearing on its broad bosom the traffic of an empire, it is a spot worthy of being rescued from the ceaseless din of the steam engine, and the lurid flames and dingy smoke of the coal furnace. But alas! the *sacra fames auri* is rapidly covering this area with private edifices; and in a few short years it is probable that the antiquary will be unable to discover a vestige of those celebrated military works, with which French and British ambition, in by-gone ages, had crowned this important and interesting point."

Beginning in 1838, when Mayor Jonas E. McClintock's proposals to build a memorial park at the Point were frustrated by the demands of river and land traffic, successive generations sought to achieve this end; the project has had more plans offered for its solution over the years than any other in the Pittsburgh region. The Point remained in modern times a blighted area containing several hundred nondescript buildings and a sprawling freight terminal that surrounded and submerged the one simple, distinguished remnant of our first days — the Blockhouse. This redoubt, one of five that originally stood on the perimeter of Fort Pitt, is the oldest authenticated structure in western Pennsylvania. Miraculously preserved since its construction in 1764, it has been saved for us by the Daughters of the American Revolution and is the brightest jewel in the new park setting.

Finally, in 1945, the Pittsburgh Regional Planning Association under the leadership of Richard K. Mellon authorized Charles M. Stotz and Ralph E. Griswold, landscape architect, to make the definitive study of the lower-triangle area that established the essential features of the park. These men were assisted by Donald M. McNeil, city traffic engineer, who did research on anticipated traffic volume and flow, and George S. Richardson, consulting engineer, who advised on the size and nature of the bridges and interchange structures, which his firm later designed in their present form. The final report and designs were presented to and approved by the Pittsburgh Regional Planning Association in November of 1945.

These plans were refined through subsequent studies by Ralph E. Griswold and John A. Renner in association with Clarke and Rapuano, landscape architects. Final designs were incorporated in plans and specifications prepared for the General State Authority by Charles M. and Edward Stotz, architect and engineer (succeeded in 1963 by Stotz, Hess and MacLachlan) in association with Griswold, Winters and Swain, landscape architects. See aerial view of park on page 90 and general park plan inside the front cover.

This successful culmination of the Point project was the product of many hands, working in harmony over the years toward a single end. Other cities and countries have marveled at the many accomplishments — of which Point Park is but one — of the guiding organization, the Allegheny Conference on Community Development, and have sent delegations to Pittsburgh or have asked that representatives of the Conference visit them, to learn how we in Pittsburgh have accomplished so much in the years since World War II. The Conference

View of the Portal from the Hilton Hotel, with Music Bastion in foreground

93

at the request of Governor Edward Martin established the Point Park Committee in 1945 to lead the Point project to its successful conclusion. Composed of leaders in business, industry, and commerce as well as the heads of city, county, and state governments, this Committee has served without personal or political prejudice or discord under the able chairmanship of Arthur B. Van Buskirk since its formation.

At the very beginning the basic decision was made to maintain a simple, unified park of monumental sweep, uncluttered by buildings and monuments or any graveyard of memorials and statues. The hills and rivers, little changed by man since the early days, provide a majestic memorial far more impressive than any man-made monument.

The park design recognizes three basic elements: the highways, the rivers, and the fort sites. While considering the aesthetic and historical aspects of the problem, it was vitally necessary to solve the needs of modern traffic and of the living city. To provide the necessary traffic interchanges it was found necessary to remove the bridges at the Point and to build new and more adequate ones some nine hundred feet upstream. Regrettably, this made the full-scale total restoration of Fort Pitt impossible, but it did provide an eighteen-acre, open park area at the Point itself and another eighteen-acre park area between the highway structures and Commonwealth Place.

The park is under the jurisdiction of the Pennsylvania Department of Forests and Waters and is properly known as Point State Park. By special arrangement, the museum within the Monongahela Bastion is administered by the Pennsylvania Historical and Museum Commission.

The aerial view on page 90 shows the plan layout of the park and its relationship to the traffic system, the downtown triangle buildings and the new buildings in the 23-acre Gateway Center, developed by the Urban Redevelopment Authority under the devoted leadership of the late David L. Lawrence during his tenures as Mayor of Pittsburgh and Governor of Pennsylvania.

Point State Park begins in front of the Hilton Hotel at Commonwealth Place, from each end of which two broad curving walkways lead to the vaulted opening known as the Portal beneath the highway. The Portal forms the sole entrance to and exit from the park for pedestrians and only those vehicles required in park maintenance. These two walkways enclose the Music Bastion of Fort Pitt, shown on page 93 and park plan inside front cover.

View from elevated Highway toward Fort Duquesne tracery and the Fountain

The ground has been excavated to expose the existing foundations of the original brick walls of Fort Pitt. A small portion of the first four feet of brick masonry has been preserved. Where foundations of buildings erected in modern times have cut away the original brick walls, they have been replaced with brick of identical character. All of the original stone footings remain in place. The visitor may enter this depressed area by a staircase and walk beside the wall. The Flag Bastion was reconstructed in 1959 (see plan inside front cover).

There is a broad plaza at the eastern end of the Portal, flanked by flags of the United States and Pennsylvania. Large forest trees have been planted on each side of the eastern face of the Portal to frame this feature of the park entrance. When the fountain has been completed it will be seen through the Portal arch on the axis of the Park. The Portal consists of three vaults, 160 feet long and 22 feet high, in the design of which Gordon Bunshaft of New York served as consulting architect. These vaults are brilliantly illuminated at night by six powerful floodlights located in ornamental basins at the bases of the vaults. The entire area below the vaults is occupied by a shallow pool with a decorative bottom formed of large river cobblestones set in a fish-scale pattern. This was done to provide an attractive appearance when the water is drained out in the winter. A slightly arched pedestrian bridge, forty feet wide, spans the pool from the eastern to the western plazas.

The illustration on page 95 shows a view toward the Point from the elevated highway. Two areas of forest trees flank the broad sweep of open lawn leading to the monumental 150-foot-high column of water formed by the fountain in its basin at the tip of the triangle. This fountain, symbolizing the water of the rivers that gave Pittsburgh its meaning, will be the very climax and principal feature of the park design.

About halfway down the open area lie the outlines of Fort Duquesne, shown by paths of stone set in the lawn. The center of this tracery is occupied by a large circular bronze marker engraved with the plan of Fort Duquesne taken from the only authentic drawing of the fort, now preserved in the Bibliotheque Nationale in Paris. The stone-paved wharf at the margin of the river has been completed for some years. Most Pittsburghers have enjoyed the concerts of the Wind Symphony and other presentations from the stone steps of the Allegheny River front. An Overlook in the western section on the left of the Portal affords a vantage point from which visitors may

Portal, Blockhouse and Monongahela Bastion, which contains the Museum

97

look over the lower park and down the Allegheny and Ohio Rivers. The monumental scale of the park had not been fully appreciated until the bridges and ramp were removed, thus permitting a full view of the broad Ohio and the hills beyond.

On page 97 may be seen a view looking back toward the city with the Portal and western Plaza on the left and, on the right, the Blockhouse which stands unchanged on its original site, and the Monongahela Bastion which contains the Fort Pitt Museum.

When the visitor reaches the western Plaza he may ascend a gentle ramp to the top of the Bastion, walk the ramparts, examine the cannon in their embrasures, and view the surrounding landscape from the same vantage point as the sentry of other days.

Landscape architects conceive the horticultural aspects of their designs in their ultimate, fully matured state. After the planting of Point State Park has been completed, it will be some years before the foliage achieves the majestic scale shown in the rendering on page 95. The great open mall shown in this picture extends from the Portal to the fountain and is bordered by trees of the species that once covered the Point when George Washington described it in 1753: ". . . a considerable Bottom of flat, well-timbered Land . . ."

These trees frame the vista of hills receding down the Ohio River. The rivers themselves are viewed intimately from the wharf promenades. Of more informal and leisurely character is the scene from the comfortable benches on the Overlook. And climaxing it all is the towering column of water in the great basin at the very tip of the Point.

These features of Point State Park are the inspired conceptions of Ralph E. Griswold, to whom must go the principal credit for the design of the park. His unflagging enthusiasm and devotion through the many years of perplexity and frustration gave heart to his fellow workers. Among his many creations in landscape design in this country and Europe, Point State Park will probably remain his masterpiece.

SUGGESTED READING LIST

From this list of books, all presently in print, the interested reader may build a library of the early history of western Pennsylvania. For a comprehensive and definitive work the reader is referred to *The Planting of Civilization in Western Pennsylvania*. For younger readers we suggest *Pioneer Life in Western Pennsylvania*. No work on the Indian has surpassed Parkman's *The Conspiracy of Pontiac*. Those who seek firsthand sources of history will relish the military records in *The Forbes Expedition*. The Fort Pitt Museum was largely based on the work "Defense in the Wilderness," a portion of *Drums in the Forest*, listed below.

Pittsburgh has three great library collections of standard and rare books on our local history: The Pennsylvania Room of the Carnegie Library, The Darlington Library of The University of Pittsburgh and the library of The Historical Society of Western Pennsylvania, which also publishes the quarterly *Western Pennsylvania Historical Magazine*.

PUBLISHED BY THE UNIVERSITY OF PITTSBURGH PRESS

Baldwin, Leland D. *The Keelboat Age on Western Waters*. Reissue 1960.

*Baldwin, Leland D. *Pittsburgh: The Story of a City*. Reissue 1970.

*Baldwin, Leland D. *Whiskey Rebels*. Reissue 1968.

Brown, Lloyd A. *Early Maps of the Ohio Valley*. 1959.

*Buck, Solon J. and Elizabeth. *The Planting of Civilization in Western Pennsylvania*. Reissue 1969.

Cleland, Hugh. *George Washington in the Ohio Valley*. 1955.

*Downes, Randolph C. *Council Fires on the Upper Ohio*. Reissue 1969.

*McCardell, Lee. *Ill-Starred General: Braddock of the Coldstream Guards* Reprint 1962.

Mulkearn, Lois, ed. *George Mercer Papers Relating to the Ohio Company of Virginia*.

Stotz, Charles Morse. *The Architectural Heritage of Western Pennsylvania*. Reissue 1966.

Wallace, Paul A. W., ed. *Thirty Thousand Miles with John Heckewelder*. 1958.

*Wright, J. E. and Doris S. Corbett. *Pioneer Life in Western Pennsylvania*. Reprint 1968.

PUBLISHED BY
THE PENNSYLVANIA HISTORICAL AND MUSEUM COMMISSION

William Penn Memorial Museum, Box 1026, Harrisburg, Pennsylvania 17108

Kent, Donald H. *The French Invasion of Western Pennsylvania, 1753*. 1954.

The Papers of Henry Bouquet, Volume II, *The Forbes Expedition*, ed. S. K. Stevens, Donald H. Kent, and Autumn L. Leonard. 1951.

*Wallace, Paul A. W. *Indians in Pennsylvania*. paper, 1968. cloth, 1970.

*At the time of printing, these books were also available in paperback editions.

BOOKS BY OTHER PUBLISHERS

Alberts, Robert C. *Adventures of Major Robert Stobo.* Houghton Mifflin Co. 1965.

Bird, Harrison. *Battle for a Continent.* Oxford University Press. 1959.

Drums in the Forest, containing "Decision at the Forks," by Alfred Procter James, and "Defense in the Wilderness," by Charles Morse Stotz. Historical Society of Western Pennsylvania. 1958 (both paper and cloth).

Hamilton, Edward P. *The French and Indian Wars.* Doubleday & Co. 1962.

The Journal of Major George Washington. Facsimile reproduction by Dominion Books, University Press of Virginia. 1963.

O'Meara, Walter. *Guns at the Forks.* Prentice-Hall. 1965.

Parkman, Francis. *The Conspiracy of Pontiac.* Everyman Edition suggested.

Peckham, Howard H. *The Colonial Wars, 1689-1762.* University of Chicago Press. 1964.

Peckham, Howard H. *Pontiac and the Indian Uprising.* Princeton University Press. 1947.

*Van Every, Dale. *Forth to the Wilderness.* William Morrow (cloth). 1962. Mentor Books-NAL (paper).

Wainwright, Nicholas B. *George Croghan, Wilderness Diplomat.* University of North Carolina Press. 1959.

Wallace, Anthony F. C. *The Death and Rebirth of the Seneca.* Knopf. 1970.

*At the time of printing, these books were also available in paperback editions.

INDEX

101

A WORD FROM THE PUBLISHERS

THE Historical Society of Western Pennsylvania, which has served this community for almost a century, welcomes the Fort Pitt Museum as a new dimension in the recorded history of Pittsburgh. The Historical Society is proud to serve as publishers of this book, the contents of which first appeared in the Society's publication, *The Western Pennsylvania Historical Magazine*. The author, Charles M. Stotz, has rearranged the text and has added numerous illustrations for this edition. The costs of publication are defrayed by a grant made to the Society by the Richard King Mellon Foundation.

As an organization which shares the concern of the Fort Pitt Museum in the field of regional history, the Historical Society welcomes to its membership all who are interested in the history of western Pennsylvania. The Society issues a quarterly magazine, arranges historical tours and river trips, provides lectures by distinguished speakers and extends the use of its unusual library at its headquarters, 4338 Bigelow Boulevard, in Pittsburgh.

C. V. STARRETT, *President*
The Historical Society of Western Pennsylvania

Pittsburgh, Pennsylvania
June 3, 1970